Attention Grabbers

for 4th–6th Graders

Zondervan/Youth Specialties Books

Adventure Games
Amazing Tension Getters
Attention Grabbers for 4th-6th Graders (Get 'Em Growing)
Called to Care
The Complete Student Missions Handbook
Creative Socials and Special Events
Divorce Recovery for Teenagers
Feeding Your Forgotten Soul
Get 'Em Talking
Good Clean Fun
Good Clean Fun, Volume 2
Great Games for 4th-6th Graders (Get 'Em Growing)
Great Ideas for Small Youth Groups
Greatest Skits on Earth
Greatest Skits on Earth, Volume 2
Growing Up in America
High School Ministry
High School TalkSheets
Holiday Ideas for Youth Groups (Revised Edition)
Hot Talks
Ideas for Social Action
Intensive Care: Helping Teenagers in Crisis
Junior High Ministry
Junior High TalkSheets
The Ministry of Nurture
On-Site: 40 On-Location Programs for Youth Groups
Option Plays
Organizing Your Youth Ministry
Play It! Great Games for Groups
Teaching the Bible Creatively
Teaching the Truth about Sex
Tension Getters
Tension Getters II
Unsung Heroes: How to Recruit and Train Volunteer Youth Workers
Up Close and Personal: How to Build Community in Your Youth Group
Youth Specialties Clip Art Book
Youth Specialties Clip Art Book, Volume 2

Attention Grabbers

for 4th-6th Graders

DAVID LYNN

Zondervan Publishing House
Grand Rapids, Michigan

Disclaimer

Like life, this book contains games that, in an unfortunate combination of circumstances, could result in emotional or physical harm. Before you use a game, you'll need to evaluate it on its own merit for your group, for its potential risk, for necessary safety precautions and advance preparation, and for possible results. Youth Specialties, Inc., Zondervan Publishing House, and David Lynn are not responsible for, nor have any control over, the use or misuse of any games published in this book.

Library of Congress Cataloging-in-Publication Data

Lynn, David, 1954–
    Attention grabbers for 4th-6th graders : terrific crowd breakers, relationship-builders and group promoters to strengthen your 8-to-12-year-olds / David Lynn.
        p.   cm.
    "Zondervan/Youth Specialties books"—P.
    "Get 'em growing from Youth Specialties."
    ISBN 0-310-52561-6
    1. Group games. 2. Intergroup relations. I. Title. II. Title: Attention grabbers for fourth-sixth graders.
GV1203.L94 1990
793'.01922—dc20   90-36534
                                                                                          CIP

All Scripture quotations, unless otherwise noted, are taken from the *Holy Bible: New International Version* (North American Edition). Copyright © 1973, 1978, 1984 by the International Bible Society. Used by permission of Zondervan Bible Publishers.

Edited by Leslie Emmons
Designed by Jack Rogers
Illustrated by Dan Pegoda
Typography by Leah Perry

Printed in the United States of America

90 91 92 93 94 95 96 97 98 99 / DP / 10 9 8 7 6 5 4 3 2 1

About the YouthSource™ Publishing Group

YOUTHSOURCE™ books, tapes, videos, and other resources pool the expertise of three of the finest youth-ministry resource providers in the world:

Campus Life Books—publishers of the award-winning *Campus Life* magazine, who for nearly fifty years have helped high schoolers live Christian lives.

Youth Specialties—serving ministers to middle-school, junior-high, and high-school youth for over twenty years through books, magazines, and training events such as the National Youth Workers Convention.

Zondervan Publishing House—one of the oldest, largest, and most respected evangelical Christian publishers in the world.

Campus Life	**Youth Specialties**	**Zondervan**
465 Gundersen Dr.	1224 Greenfield Dr.	1415 Lake Dr. S.E.
Carol Stream, IL 60188	El Cajon, CA 92021	Grand Rapids, MI 49506
708/260-6200	619/440-2333	616/698-6900

To my birth children
Amy Kathryn and Megan Elizabeth

Table of Contents

Acknowledgments

The attention grabbers in this collection are a compilation of a wide variety of activities suitable for the upper elementary grades. Many of these activities originally appeared in the *Ideas* library published by Youth Specialties, Inc. I would like to thank all the creative people responsible for developing and testing these activities. Without their dedication to young people, this book of attention grabbers would not have been possible.

How To Use Attention Grabbers

Attention Grabbers are games and activities that capture the attention of young people. They are a creative, entertaining, and engaging way to establish fun and playful climates in which groups of kids can learn and grow. Why use them with your group?

Attention grabbers set a mood for learning that is fun and relaxed. They serve as excellent mixers, breaking down barriers and getting things moving.

Attention grabbers are "stress busters." They help your kids unwind before you begin an important lesson. Believe it or not, stress is an issue for nine-year-olds as well as twelve-year-olds. Talk with elementary and middle-school teachers, and you will hear stories of uptight and tense children. Kids are experiencing more stress because their parents and other adults are experiencing more stress.

Attention grabbers provide older children with an opportunity to test out—in a safe environment—their emerging friendship skills. Upper-elementary-school children find friendship clusters more important than younger kids do. They begin to take an interest in the opposite sex, and spending time with friends and having best friends are important to them. The interactions created through the use of attention grabbers offer kids the chance to relate to others in an enjoyable and non-threatening environment.

Attention grabbers are great rapport builders. Adults working with this age group too often expect kids to listen to them simply because they are adults. But adults today must earn the right to be heard by kids. As you get actively involved with your group, your kids will begin to trust and bond with you, and they will listen to you when it comes time for the educational component of your program.

What are the attention grabbers in this book?

Groupers. Overcome the difficulties of breaking into groups for study or selecting teams for play by making a game out of "getting grouped." Turn this usually tough task into a fun activity with these games, or simply play them as fun crowd breakers.

Mixer Mania. These attention grabbers are designed to provide opportunities for your group members to interact and have some fun at the same time. Get your group mingling with Mixer Mania!

Getting-To-Know-You Stuff. When you need an activity to help your kids become better acquainted, try one of these attention grabbers. Whether it's learning names or learning about each other, these attention grabbers work well.

Crazy Crowd Breakers. These attention grabbers are intended for performance. They are designed for laughter and entertainment, not for humor at someone's expense. If the people chosen to participate in these zany activities are "good sports" and their leader uses the activities skillfully, the results will be very positive and lots of fun.

Group Engagers. The attention grabbers found here involve all of your group members. They are designed to produce both laughter and interaction. Use them as crowd breakers and meeting starters when you want group participation.

Skits That Grab. Try one of these hilarious skits at your next retreat, camp, or group meeting. Skits are great introductory activities and create a fun, casual atmosphere.

Music Madness. For some unusual ways to use music to grab your group's attention, try one of these activities.

Servant Events. Older elementary-age kids can be, and *need* to be, involved in service projects. Here are a few creative ideas for engaging your group in missions and Christian service.

Relationship Builders. These creative caring-and-sharing experiences build positive relationships among young people and between adults and young people. They are not meant to be used as meeting starters or crowd breakers, but rather as community-building experiences.

Group Promoters. Here you will find some creative publicity and promotion ideas designed to get your kids' attention and build up your adult leadership.

Bible Brain Teasers. Here are some creative attention grabbers designed to challenge, as well as entertain, your kids.

Mindbenders. Mental games are wonderful fun even if your kids can't always figure them out—adults can't either! Introduce one now and then to challenge your group's thinking skills. Pace yourself with Mindbenders, as they tend to take a little longer than other types of attention grabbers.

**Teaching Kids (And Adults)
How To Have Fun**

We all have heard the saying, "It's not how you play the game; it's whether you"—uh, wait a minute. Somewhere along the way, "How you play the game" was lost. Yet, *how* the game is played is *why* attention grabbers are needed. Recapturing an attitude of play can be difficult, but here are a few tips that can help you make a playful "attitude adjustment" within your group.

Be patient. In an effort to appear "cool" and "with it," some kids today try to cultivate a certain avant-garde attitude that prohibits them from having fun. Others become so preoccupied with winning that the joy of play is lost. Don't assume your group will automatically embrace a new philosophy of having fun just because you've used an attention grabber or two. It may take time for them to lose their "cool" attitude, so be patient.

Model fun and enthusiasm by example. A new attitude toward fun and games will more likely be "caught" than "taught." This means that you must start by changing the way the adults in your group feel about attention grabbers before the kids will change. Young people learn more from watching than from listening. If your adult leaders sit on the sidelines during an activity in which kids are expected to be involved, your young people will be more likely to opt out of participation, too. If your adult leaders push the kids to win, the games will be tense and competitive. If, however, your adult leaders jump in and get involved in the fun, their excitement will be contagious.

As an adult leader, don't miss out on important opportunities to teach young people how to have fun—by your example. And involve other adult leaders in the fun play. When they stand along the sidelines, grab their hands and pull them into play. And if they become too competitive, gently remind them of the reason you are celebrating with play.

Create an atmosphere of healthy competition. The best games and activities are those that rely on "unskilled competition," competition that involves *all* of your kids and not just the athletes. This means that all players are given equal chances to participate and succeed. At this age, in particular, such opportunities are crucial.

Use your attention grabbers to build self-esteem. Don't emphasize winning and losing. If you do have winners and losers, approach the concept in a way that makes the whole group feel good about the game's outcome. With certain games and activities, having winning teams is appropriate, especially if team effort is involved. Any awards or rewards given to winners should be sharable.

Explain your attention grabber clearly and quickly. When you introduce a game or activity to your group, get everyone's attention first. This is by extending an invitation for everyone to play. Assure players through gesture and tone of voice that the game will be fun and will build them up.

Be certain that all the participants are able to see you and hear your instructions. Give the name of the game or activity, explain step-by-step how to play or what to do, and then give a demonstration with another participant.

If the attention grabber is a game, play a practice round before you begin in earnest. This assures the group that you want to focus on fun rather than on winning or losing. A trial run also builds trust in the play process and in the group.

Don't get so caught up in the explanation of a game or activity that you take it too seriously. Getting angry with participants because they don't understand the rules or instructions should be a signal to move on to another game or activity.

If the activity you are explaining requires teamwork, divide the group before you explain the activity. And if the activity requires the kids to be in a circle, form one before presenting it. This makes the transition from explanation to demonstration and the practice round much easier.

Choosing the Right Attention Grabber for Your Group

All of the attention grabbers in this book can be played by young people in grades four, five, and six. Between ages eight and twelve, children grow in their skills and abilities. Their speed and endurance increase, and their imaginations and creativity expand. They are becoming more interested in working together as a group and in collaborating with peers and adults to achieve a common goal. Team games and competition become more enjoyable. But because kids are interested in playing games and participating in activities does not necessarily mean that *any* game or activity will do. Keep the following factors in mind as you select attention grabbers from this or any other book.

Decide upon a purpose. Obviously, we use attention grabbers so that kids can have fun. It is valuable, however, to look at other reasons for using them. Perhaps you want your group to become better acquainted, to burn off energy, or to learn team cooperation or a new truth. All of these purposes can be achieved using attention grabbers. Know your purpose before you select an attention grabber. And remember, it's okay occasionally to play games and do activities simply for their enjoyment (Proverbs 17:22).

Include all group members. One of the mistakes adults make as they choose games and activities is falling into the "personality trap." Leaders often choose activities and games that the popular, sharp-looking, athletic kids will like. The responses of these kids become the litmus test for an activity's or a game's success or failure. But in the process of catering to such kids, we can neglect the needs of the other kids in our groups. Select a wide variety of activities for your program. Give each group member the opportunity to be "It," to select a favorite game or activity, or to be a Safety Guard.

Involve your group members in your choices. Young people, in partnership with adults, need to make programming decisions. This does not mean that adult leaders abdicate their adult responsibilities and allow kids to make all of the decisions. Rather, choose *together* activities and games that you both wish to do or play.

Make adequate preparations. When you choose an attention grabber, remember that some require preparation on your (or the participants') part. Pick those for which you can adequately prepare. That doesn't mean you should always settle for attention grabbers that require little or no preparation; take time to play those that need some "prep time." The results are usually worth the extra time and effort.

Adjust your attention grabbers for the physically challenged. Mentally retarded, handicapped, and other physically challenged young people are entitled to be included in the fun.

Involve physically challenged young people to the extent they are able to participate. With some imagination and prayer, you can find creative ways to include all of your kids. But as you make modifications to accommodate the physically challenged, think of safety first!

Go easy on food activities. Games and activities requiring the use of food should not be played unless the food is going to be eaten. For example, playing with eggs that will most likely be broken and thrown away gives young people who live in a world where so many people go to bed hungry every night the wrong message.

Maintain final authority. You are the final authority when it comes to game and activity selection. You know your young people better than anyone else does. It is ultimately up to you to make the decision about which activities will be best for your kids. Just because an attention grabber is printed in a book does not mean it's suitable or safe for your group. Remember to use the ideas and activities that fit your group's particular personality, locale, size, playing space, and ages. And don't be afraid to try something new once in a while.

Creating Play

Play does not just happen; it is created. Leaders must create an environment where an attitude of play can flourish. As you work to develop this attitude within your group, consider the following elements.

The game is for the kids, not the other way around. Don't allow a game or activity to control its players. Empower your kids with the right attitude and the skills to control an activity or game. On one occasion our group was doing the "Forty-Inch Dash" (see page 44). One of the group members suggested we use

hard candies instead of marshmallows and a new game was born. Flexibility is the key.

Safety First (and Second and Third)

Safety is a *must* for every youth-group leader. Use common sense as you select games, choose equipment, decide on places in which to play, involve adults, and play the games. If the game or activity doesn't feel safe, assume it's not, and don't play!

One of the best ways to ensure safety is to play the game yourself before trying it with your kids. This will help you to know what to look for as your group plays the game or does the activity.

Most important to the safety success of any game is the use of Safety Guards. A Safety Guard is a "referee plus." Some Guards referee the games, some lead the games, and others participate in play. But all of them must be safety conscious at all times. They need to be prepared for their role; for a good start, have them read this chapter.

Safety Guards are given ultimate authority when it comes to running a game or activity. If they see play getting out of hand, they can call a Time-Out. If they see players participating irresponsibly, they can talk with them one-on-one about safety.

Older kids can also act as Safety Guards. It's best to designate a different young person as a Safety Guard for each game played. Rotating the responsibility around the group helps kids recognize their personal stake in safety and helps them take safety more seriously.

The following five safety checks can help you and your Safety Guards create a fun and enjoyable playing experience.

1. Boundaries of play should be clearly marked and delineated.
2. The playing area should be clear of debris and other hazards. Also, players need to remove watches, jewelry, pencils, or anything else that could hurt them or others during play.
3. Make sure that the object of the game and its rules are clearly understood by all players. Too often, players will nod their heads in agreement indicating they understand the rules without really comprehending them.
4. All players should be allowed to take a personal Time-Out at any time during play. Anyone who is out of breath or feeling threatened by a game needs the freedom to walk away from play.
5. Make sure you have enough Safety Guards for each activity. And don't assign anyone to the role of Safety Guard before they are prepared.

Plan for the unexpected. If you are scheduling an outdoor event, plan for weather changes. Prepare a few indoor activities in case of rain, sleet, hail, or "gloom of night." The mood and interest level of your group is as unpredictable as the weather. Overplan rather than underplan. What works with your kids one month may not work the next. Have extra games planned to spark their interest when things begin to slow down.

Timing is everything. When you try to decide how much time to allow for a game, use the energy and "fun level" of your group as an indicator. Don't end a game when players are bored with it; it is better to end while players are still having fun so they will want to play the game again. On the other hand, don't end games so soon that some kids miss out on having fun.

Another dimension of timing is to use it as a part of the game experience. In some games, a shortened time limit can add to the excitement. Adjust the timing to the level of the group. If players become overwhelmed or frustrated, lengthen the time limitation, and if the activity is too easy, shorten it.

There are no such things as "official rules." In fact, strict adherence to a set of rules can be harmful to upper-elementary-age young people. This is the stage at which kids learn about the flexibility and relativity of rules, a skill that is foundational to more complex learning. Giving children the opportunity to change the rules or create new rules is quite healthy. You may have observed young people at play where one child says, "Last one to the house is *It*." Whereupon another child retorts, "Not included!" and the first child shouts, "No say-backs." This is an example of children using their new-found ability to manipulate rules.

Changing the rules or creating new ones is also a great way to energize a game. By modifying rules, players are in actuality creating new and different games. Point out to kids that by changing rules and modifying games they are taking charge of creating their own play. Rule changes need to be agreed upon as a group before play begins, of course.

A New Attitude Toward Winning and Losing

Many games have winners and losers and the reality is that in most games and activities, some participants do consistently better than others. As leaders, we can help redefine and refocus the win/

lose concept.

Take advantage of teachable moments. Occasionally, after an activity or play event, discuss what happened. In a positive way, talk with the group about what they learned from the activity. Emphasize the need for players to do their best rather than to prove they are better than everyone else.

Another way to redefine winning and losing is through the use of teams. Team winning is different than individual winning because to win requires cooperation and team effort. And the team that does not win, does so also as a team.

Scoring is another means by which you can refocus the win/lose concept. Traditionally, it has had the effect of focusing play on the outcome—who wins and who loses. You can create a new challenge and a whole new spirit to game playing by changing the way you score. Try giving points for things players would not expect: the funniest mishap, the most creative modification of the rules, or the the best team cooper-

ation, for example.

Scoring also can be changed through the ways points are distributed. Instead of giving one point at a time, try giving out 10 points, or 100. Kids will want to play their best when they can get 100 or 1,000 points. Keep the spread between points small so that the last-place team or person is still fairly close to the first place. For example, with three teams, first place may be 500 points; second place 475 and third place 450. That way, the team in last still gets lots of points and feels a sense of achievement.

Finally, train your Safety Guards to referee events so that competition is equalized. They can do this by focusing more intently on infractions by the winning teams or individuals, and by being more lenient with the teams that are behind. The players will soon realize that the Safety Guards are consistently taking the side of the underdogs. After a while, players will focus more on having fun than on earning points or keeping score.

Groupers

Overcome the difficulties of breaking into groups for study or selecting teams for play by making a game out of "getting grouped." Turn this usually tough task into a fun activity with these games, or simply play them as fun crowd breakers.

Bagged Teams

Place the names of all the players together in a bag or sack. Mix them up. The leader draws the first two names. These two players are now the captains of opposing teams or different groups, and the two of them take turns selecting names from the bag of other players to be on their teams or in their groups. It's okay to be chosen last in this fashion because the choice was random.

Barnyard

Give each person a folded piece of paper with the name of one of six different animals (pig, horse, cow, chicken, duck, dog) written on it. The players are not to say a word or to look at the paper. They are to sit down and wait for further instructions. (To ensure equal groups or teams, assign the same animal name to every sixth person.) After everyone is seated, they look at their animal name.

The lights are turned out and everyone immediately stands up and makes the sounds of their animals.

As soon as players find others making the same noise, they lock arms and try to find other teammates. In no time, the players will be divided into six groups. When the lights come back on, they should sit down with their animal groups. You can combine three of the groups into one to get two teams, or combine two teams into one, so that you have three teams. Add or subtract animal names from the list to make Barnyard work to select any number of groups.

Birthday Barnyard

If you are working with a large group, this one may work well for you. Give each person a list like the one below or post the list somewhere in a readily visible spot in the room. After everyone is seated and has received a copy of the list, instruct them to look at the sound or action described for their birth month. When the lights go out, they are to immediately stand up and make the appropriate sounds or actions. As soon as they find others doing the same things and making the same sounds, they lock arms with them and look for the rest of their teammates, all the time continuing their sounds or actions. As soon as all the birthday groups are together, they sit down, and your large group is then broken into twelve smaller groups.

January	Shout "Happy New Year!"
February	Say "Be my Valentine."
March	Blow (wind)
April	Hop (Easter Bunny)
May	Say "Mother, may I?" (Mother's Day)
June	Say "School's out!"
July	Make fireworks sounds
August	Sing "Take me out to the ball game"
September	Make falling noises (autumn)
October	Say "Trick or treat!"
November	Say "Gobble, gobble"
December	Say "Ho Ho Ho, Merrrry Christmas!"

Birthday Shuffle

This icebreaker activity starts out like musical chairs. Ask everyone to sit in sturdy chairs in a big circle. There should be one extra person in the middle of the circle, without a chair. This person is "It" and calls out any three months of the year. Everyone in the circle whose birthday is in one of those months must get up and find a new chair. While they're scrambling to find new seats, "It" tries to sit in a vacant chair. Whoever is left without a chair becomes the new "It." When "It" calls out, "Happy Birthday!" everyone must get up and find other seats.

When you are ready to get into groups, call out the names of the months that you want in groups and send each to a designated area. For example, if you want four groups, simply point to a corner of the room and say, "January, February, March—over there." Then point to another corner of the room and say, "April, May, June—over there." Do this until you have your four groups.

Domino Teams

Design large index cards to look like dominos. Create as many sets as you plan to have teams or groups, each set on a different color. Put as many dots as you plan to have teammates or group members (i.e., four groups of seven people would have sets of cards in red, blue, green, and black, with cards of one dot through seven respectively). Tape the cards on the backs of players as they come in and then explain, "At the whistle you are to discover what your domino numbers and colors are. You may ask questions of those around you, but they may answer only with a YES or a NO. You may only ask one question per person. When you find out what your domino is, go to your team or group area." Areas should be designated prior to the start of the activity. Eventually, you will get all your teams or groups in the right areas and everyone will have fun in the process.

For Better or For Verse

Here is a way to use scripture to divide into groups. Before you get together with your group, write out different verses, phrase by phrase, on separate three-by-five cards. To identify the verse, write the book on one card and the chapter and verse on another. Randomly distribute the cards and let the kids form the verses. Each group is created by the kids who hold cards from the same verse. If you want six groups of five kids each (you can also assign adults to each group by giving them one of the cards), then you will need six different verses with each of the verses broken down into five different parts. Examples are shown in the diagram on the next page.

PROVERBS	3:5	TRUST IN THE LORD	WITH ALL YOUR HEART	AND LEAN NOT ON YOUR OWN UNDERSTANDING.
1 JOHN	4:19	WE LOVE	BECAUSE HE FIRST	LOVED US.
GALATIANS	5:16	SO I SAY, LIVE BY THE SPIRIT,	AND YOU WILL NOT GRATIFY	THE DESIRES OF THE SINFUL NATURE

Gather By . . .

One of the worst methods of choosing teams is that of selecting two captains who then take turns picking their friends. How about trying this one for a change of pace?

The leader asks the players to gather into groups based upon certain characteristics like the following:

1. "Gather by the school you attend." If there are too many schools, you can combine them to form more equal teams.
2. "Gather by birthday." All players born on odd-numbered days on one team, and all players born on even-numbered days on the other.
3. "Gather by the first letter of the player's last name (A-L; M-Z)." If you need more teams, break up the alphabet accordingly.
4. "Gather by birth month." You can then combine the months to form the number of teams you need.
5. "Gather by hair color."
6. "Gather by eye color."
7. "Gather by sock color."
8. "Gather by bubble-gum flavor." For this one, distribute sticks of flavored gum just before you begin. If you want four teams, pass out equal numbers of four flavors.

When teams are not equal, select several players to move and make them even.

Group Detectives

This grouper works best with a crowd of twenty-five or more. The basic idea is to have everyone gather into a specified group as *quickly* as possible. These groups should be based on common characteristics or descriptions. For example, you might start with: "See how fast you can get into groups of people with the same first initial." At the end of a time limit, check to see how the groups did and make sure that there is only one group for each letter. Then, move on to a new group description and try to beat the time set by the previous round; or, as the activity progresses, keep trying to set record times. When you like the group divisions, begin their study time or go on to play team games.

Some other categories to gather by:

1. Those who have the same number of people in their immediate families.
2. Those who have the same favorite colors.
3. Those who like the same subjects in school.
4. Those who have the same color eyes.
5. Those wearing the same color shirts or blouses.
6. Those who are the same ages.
7. Those who are in the same grades.
8. Those wearing the same color socks.
9. Those with the same color hair.
10. Those who have the same favorite sports.

Mother Goose Pairs

As group members arrive, give them "Mother Goose" character names or sayings printed on three-by-five cards. Then ask the kids to find the other halves of their Mother Goose rhymes. When they are done you will have the kids in pairs. If you want four, six, or more pairs per group, duplicate the Mother Goose pairs to suit your needs. For example, if you want groups of six, hand out three copies of each Mother Goose pair. The following is a list of rhymes with the pairs of characters or sayings.

1. LITTLE BO-PEEP—Little Bo-Peep; Sheep.
2. PAT-A-CAKE—Pat-a-Cake; Baker's man.
3. JACK JUMPED OVER THE CANDLESTICK—Jack; Candlestick.
4. HUSH-A-BYE—Baby; Cradle.
5. SIMPLE SIMON—Simple Simon; Pieman.
6. THREE BLIND MICE—Three blind mice; Farmer's wife.
7. MISS MUFFET—Miss Muffet; Curds and whey.
8. HUMPTY DUMPTY—Humpty Dumpty; King's men.
9. OLD MOTHER HUBBARD—Old Mother Hubbard; Poor dog.
10. JACK AND JILL—Jack and Jill; Pail of water.
11. ROBIN HOOD—Robin Hood; Little John.
12. BAA, BAA, BLACK SHEEP—Black

sheep; Wool.
13. THE CAT AND THE FIDDLE—Cat and the fiddle; Cow jumped over the moon.
14. THE MULBERRY BUSH—Mulberry Bush; Cold and frosty morning.
15. TOM, TOM, THE PIPER'S SON—Tom, Tom; The piper's son.
16. MARY, MARY, QUITE CONTRARY—Mary, Mary; How does your garden grow?
17. LITTLE JACK HORNER—Jack Horner; Pulled out a plum.
18. PETER THE PUMPKIN EATER—Peter, Peter; Pumpkin eater.
19. RING-A-ROUND THE ROSEY—A pocketful of posies; We all fall down.
20. PETER PIPER—Peter Piper; Peck of pickled peppers.
21. THERE WAS AN OLD WOMAN—Old woman; Lived in a shoe.
22. LITTLE BOYS—What are little boys made of? Puppy dog's tails.
23. LITTLE GIRLS—What are little girls made of? Sugar and spice.
24. LITTLE TOM TUCKER—Tom Tucker; Sings for his supper.
25. LONDON BRIDGE—London Bridge; Falling down.

Painter's Caps

Have you tried every possible way to distinguish teams from each other—headbands, armbands, balloons tied to wrists? Try dyed painter's caps—you can keep them from event to event or give them to the kids as mementos.

Most paint stores carry inexpensive cloth painter's caps. Soak them in dye for ten to fifteen minutes, then tumble dry each color separately. The brighter the colors, the more distinct the teams will be from each other when they play games. Hand the caps out to kids as they arrive—each kid getting a color different from the kid before—and when all your players have arrived, the teams are divided.

Puzzle Grouper

Collect as many different magazine covers as you want groups or teams. Create a jigsaw puzzle out of each one. You should cut as many puzzle pieces per magazine cover as you want people in a group or on a team. As young people arrive, give them each a piece of one of the puzzles. Tell them not to show their puzzle pieces to anyone. When you are ready to begin, ask the kids to—as quickly as possible—put their puzzles together by identifying other kids who have pieces of the same magazine cover. Once they have put their puzzles together, group members should sit down as a unit.

Shuffle the Deck

Here's a simple, lively way to divide a large group into teams. Distribute a deck of playing cards to the group, one per player. Then call out different combinations, such as:

- "Get in a group that adds up to fifty-eight."
- "Find three people of the same suit."
- "Find five numbers in a row, of any suit."
- "Find your whole suit."

- "Find four of you: four threes, four eights."

For larger groups, use multiple decks of cards; for smaller groups, eliminate some cards. Then create your own combinations.

Streets and Alleys

This is a great game to use to get large groups seated in rows. One person is "It" and chases a runner through a maze of people formed in the manner shown in the diagram.

Everyone in the maze is facing in one direction with their hands joined, forming "alleys." When "Streets" is called, all do a right face and grasp hands once more. The person who is "It" tries to catch the runner but cannot cross the joined hands. When "Alleys" is called, everyone in the maze assumes their original position. When you are done playing, ask the players to sit down right where they are.

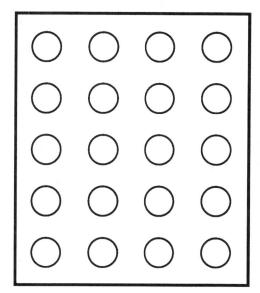

Thumbs-Up Tradition

You can begin a tradition with your group that will be a fun and easy way to choose "It." When the leader clenches her or his fist with a thumb high in the air, players follow suit. The last player with a thumb up in the air begins the game as "It."

CHAPTER 3

Mixer Mania

Looking for activities to get your group mingling? These attention grabbers are designed to provide opportunities for your group members to interact and have some fun at the same time.

Balloon Stomp

Here's a great activity for older kids. Everyone receives a blown-up balloon with an eighteen-inch piece of string tied to its stem. Players tie their balloon around their ankle with the string. When the game begins, they try to stomp and pop everyone else's balloon, while keeping their own intact. For added fun, give players two balloons and have them attach one to each ankle. Be sure to have players remove their shoes before beginning.

Bean Blitz

This is a good way to get kids involved with each other at the beginning of a meeting. Give all of the kids envelopes containing twenty beans or pennies. They then circulate around the room offering others the opportunity to guess the number of pennies or beans in their closed hands. They approach others and say, "Odd or Even?" If the approached persons guess correctly, they get the beans or the pennies. If they guess incorrectly, they must give up the same number. Set a time limit and enjoy the fun.

Blind Sardines

Here's a good game that is not only fun, but community building. There are no winners or losers in the traditional sense. All you need is a large room and blindfolds for everyone.

One person is appointed "sardine." The sardine does not wear a blindfold. All the other kids wear blindfolds and their objective is to come into contact with the sardine. When a person wearing a blindfold touches someone else, the "toucher" asks if the person touched is the sardine. The sardine must say "Yes" if touched. Once players touch the sardine, they must hold onto the sardine for the remainder of the game, so that a chain of people is gradually formed. If players touch anyone in the chain, it's as if they touched the sardine, and then can add themselves to the chain. The sardine must not attempt to avoid being touched but is free to walk about the room. The game concludes when all players are part of the chain.

Crows and Cranes

Divide the group into two teams. Players on one side are "Crows," and those on the other are "Cranes." The two teams line up facing each other on two lines four or five feet apart. The leader flips a coin (heads for "Crows" and tails for "Cranes") and calls out the name of the team that won the toss. If "Crows" is called out, the "Crows" must turn around and run, with the "Cranes" in hot pursuit. If any of the "Cranes" succeed in touching any of the "Crows" before they cross a given line (fifteen to thirty feet away), they are considered captives of the "Cranes" and must aid the "Cranes" when play continues. The team that captures all the members of the other team is the winner.

Duckie Wuckie

Everyone sits in a circle with "It" in the middle. "It" is blindfolded and has a rolled-up newspaper (loosely rolled so as not to hurt anyone). "It" is spun around as everyone else silently changes seats. The person blindfolded then finds a person's lap only by using the end of the newspaper. Once a lap is found, the newspaper is unrolled and placed in front of the person. "It" sits on the newspaper and says, "Duckie Wuckie." In a disguised voice, the person behind "It" responds, "Quack-Quack." ("Duckie Wuckie" and "Quack-Quack" may be repeated twice more.) After each "Quack-Quack" the blindfolded person may guess the identity of the player quacking. If the guess is correct, the quacking player removes the blindfold; if incorrect, "It" must find another lap and try again.

Here's a good mixer, one that really gets people talking and mingling. Type up index cards with statements like those listed below. The words in italics are typed onto the smaller right-hand portion of the card, which is then cut off (see illustration). If you tear the cards, make sure your kids can't match the torn ends like a jigsaw puzzle. Prevent this by tearing the cards into two sections, then again tearing one of the ends so that the two sections can't be matched up.

A sample list of phrases:

I always eat bacon *with my eggs.*

Tarzan lived in the jungle with his wife *Jane.*

I like peanut butter and jelly sandwiches with *lots of jelly.*

It is not polite to burp at the *dinner table.*

Teachers get mad when you pass notes *in class.*

Moms always tell you to eat your *vegetables.*

I always eat bacon   *with my eggs.*

Peanut butter sticks to the roof *of your mouth.*

No one should spit into the *wind.*

Why did the chicken cross the *road*?

Put your money where your *mouth is.*

Bus drivers always yell, *"Shut up!"*

Smoking is dangerous to your *health.*

The best part of school is *recess.*

Adults sometimes think they know *everything.*

Parents don't give kids enough *allowance money.*

The large and small portions of the cards are handed out at random, with the instructions that players are to find the correct match-ups to their portions. They must do this by going up to others, introducing themselves, and then holding their cards together and reading them out loud.

Some combinations are very funny. If two people think they have a match, they must check with the designated leader who has all the correct answers. If they have a match, they can sit down.

Name Guess

On slips of paper write names of famous people or characters that your kids know (Bible characters, cartoon characters, sports figures, TV personalities, and so forth) and pin one to the back of each person without letting them see who they are. Players ask other group members questions that can be answered either YES or NO to help them guess their own identities. When group members discover their identities, they should continue to mingle, answering the questions of those not yet sure of their famous persons.

Page Scramble

Give each team captain a children's storybook with titles such as *Waldo the Jumping Dragon* or *Big Albert Moves into Town*. The cornier the better. You can get inexpensive, used children's storybooks at good second-hand bookstores. Make sure each book has the same number of pages. Before passing the books out, carefully remove the pages from each book cover and mix them up so that each team has a book with the correct *number* of pages but not the correct pages. On a signal, the teams' captains distribute the pages among team members and they begin trading page for page with other teams. The whole place becomes a giant trading floor. The first team to put together a completed book, with all its pages in order, wins.

The Situation Game

If you have your group sitting around in a circle or in rows of chairs, this fun game will liven things up. Have the kids whisper their identities in the ears of the people sitting to their right. They should be as creative as possible with this, telling their neighbors *who they are*—Batman, a Teenage Mutant Ninja Turtle, or Wonder Woman, for examples. Then have them tell the people to their left *where they are*. These should be funny also—places like "In the bathtub," or "On top of the school." Warn the group that their responses must be tasteful. Have them mix up, find new seats, and tell their new neighbors to the right *what they are wearing*, and the people to their left *what they are doing*. After all this is done, have each person tell who they are, where they are, what they are wearing, and what they are doing. They tell the things that the other people to their left and right told them. Such as, "My name is Spider Man. I'm at the mall; I'm wearing a Ninja outfit and doing jumping jacks." If you have a large crowd, ask only a few to tell their stories or ask for a few volunteers.

Tug 'Em Out

This is a wild game that is easy to play, but needs careful monitoring for safety when it is played with younger kids. All the boys get inside a circle and huddle together in any position, locking arms. The girls attempt to tug the boys out of the circle in any way they can. The guys cannot fight back; they can only hold on to the other guys and try to stay in the huddle as long as possible.

Zoo

Ask the group to sit in a circle, and have one less chair than there are people. The extra person stands in the middle as the Zookeeper. Everyone is assigned the name of an animal. The Zookeeper begins by calling out several of the animal names and the people with those animal names must exchange chairs. At the same time, the Zookeeper tries to sit in one of the vacated chairs. The person who fails to get a chair becomes the new Zookeeper. The Zookeeper also has the option of calling out "Zoo," at which time all of the players must exchange chairs.

Be sure to use sturdy chairs—this game is really wild and can result in kids landing in each other's laps. Also, be sure to emphasize fun and safety before this game begins and have an appointed Safety Guard monitor the action.

CHAPTER 4

Getting-To-Know-You Stuff

When you need an activity to help your kids become better acquainted, try one of these attention grabbers. Whether it's learning names or learning about each other, these attention grabbers work well.

Back Snatching

This is a good way to get everybody acquainted. Pin a name onto each kid's back (either phoney names, middle names, or real names if the kids don't know each other.) At a given signal, the kids start copying names off the backs of the other kids, while at the same time trying to keep people from copying the names off their own backs. This results in a lot of twisting, turning, and trying to keep backs from being seen. The object is to get the longest list of names.

Community Quiz

This crowd breaker works great as a mixer. It's most effective in situations where you will know everyone in attendance. You will need to contact each person in advance, get certain information from them, and then include that information in a written quiz that you print up before your meeting or event.

The quiz should contain the same number of multiple choice or true-false questions as there are people (or you could have more than one question for each person).

You can then use the quiz one of several ways. One way is to simply give everyone copies and have them begin milling around the room, asking each other for the information needed to answer the questions correctly. At the end of a time limit, whoever has the most correct answers wins. Another way would be to have the kids take the test first and then have them stand up and give the correct answers to the questions that are about them. Either way works fine, although the first suggestion is more active and requires more group interaction. One way to combine both would be to have everyone take the test first, and then mill around the room asking each other for the correct answers to see if they were right or wrong.

The key is to compose questions that are humorous and interesting and that include little-known personal facts. This way, the questionnaire is not only fun, but is also very informative.

Some sample questions:

1. Danny Thompson is saving his money to buy:
   a. a bike.
   b. a dictionary.
   c. a trumpet.
   d. a new skateboard.
2. Lisa Burns hates:
   a. sardines.
   b. artichokes.
   c. cranberries.
   d. pizza.
3. Bill Florden's dad once appeared on "The Johnny Carson Show."
   a. True.
   b. False.
4. Next Christmas, Paula Lovik's family is going:
   a. to stay home.
   b. to Aspen, Colorado.
   c. to her grandmother's house in Memphis.
   d. crazy.

Drop the Blankie

This is a great way to get everyone better acquainted. Before starting, make sure visitors are introduced, so that everyone has at least heard everyone else's name. Divide into two teams and have them huddle at opposite ends of the room. Two people (neutral) hold a blanket in a vertical position, fully opened and touching the floor. Each team sends one person to stand twelve inches from their side of the blanket. When they are ready, the blanket is dropped. Whichever player says the other player's name cor-

rectly first, captures that other person, and the losing player changes teams. The game continues until one team has only one person remaining. When nei-

ther player knows the other's name, they are introduced and sent back to their teams.

Guess Who

For an easy get-acquainted activity, ask each young person to write down something about themselves that probably no one else knows. If they have trouble coming up with a unique contribution, suggest unusual pets they might have, or weird snacks or sandwiches that they like. If you get really desperate, ask for their mothers' middle names. Collect all the responses.

Next, instruct the kids to listen to the clues as you read them and try to guess the persons they think the clues identify. Give 1,000 points for each correct guess, and have everyone keep score for themselves. For a prize, give away a copy of the church directory or an address book, so the winner can write in the facts learned about people in the group.

Identity

As the young people enter the room, have them each fill out name tags and drop them in a basket. After everyone has arrived, have them circle up. Pass the basket around and have everyone take name tags (not their own) without letting others see the names.

Then have everyone turn to the left and place the name tags they are holding on the backs of the persons standing in front of them. The object of the game is to discover the names printed on the name tags pinned to their backs. The players find out their identities by

asking questions that can be answered with a "Yes" or "No" (Questions like, "Do I have red hair?" or, "Am I wearing jeans?"). Players can ask only two questions of each person they meet.

When the kids discover whose names they are wearing, they then go to those individuals, place their hands on their shoulders and proceed to follow them around the room. As more people discover their identities, the lines of people with hands on shoulders will lengthen until the last person finds the right name tag.

Match Tag

Give everyone name tags with things written on them like favorite colors, favorite musical groups, favorite movies

of this year, favorite TV shows, favorite places in town to eat, and so on. The kids write in their answers and then put on the tags. After everyone has filled out their tags, they all try to find other participants whose choices exactly match or are most like theirs and pair up.

My Most Embarrassing Balloon

Assemble your group members so they are two or three feet apart. Blow up an extra-large balloon, and—while you pinch its neck—tell the kids that every time the balloon is released and comes to rest, the kids nearest it must tell the group the funniest or most embarrassing things that have ever happened to

them. Let the kids know that they should be thinking of their funny situations right away rather than waiting for the balloon.

Then let the balloon go. While the first victim is thinking, a nearby kid should blow up the balloon in order to release it after the brief narration. This icebreaker works best when it continues rapid-fire, so keep it moving.

Name Game

Before the party or meeting, look up in a name-your-baby book the first names of all the students who will attend. Write each name's original meaning on a card and distribute to your adult leaders answer keys that match meanings with names. Lay out the cards on a table and, when the kids arrive, ask them to choose the cards that they believe reflect the meanings of their names.

Those who choose incorrectly must trade with others until they all hold their own name's meanings. Then, in pairs, students should answer at least these

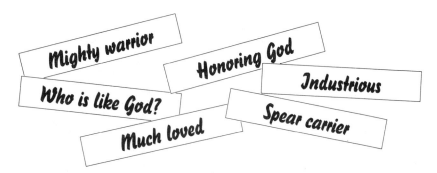

questions for each other:

- How do you feel about the meaning of your name?
- Why were you given the name you have (e.g., were you named after a relative or family friend)?
- Where would you someday like to see your name (e.g., on a building, in a book, on a screen)?

After five minutes or so of sharing, regroup the students and ask them to introduce each other with the information they discovered. You may want to give them this pattern to follow:

"My friend here is Jonathan; his name means 'gift of Jehovah,' which he thinks is hot. He was named for an uncle, and someday he'd like to see his name in a book."

Scrambled Name

Here is a little game that works well as a mixer when groups are large (fifteen or more) and when people don't know each other. Give everyone pieces of paper and pencils, and write their names down with the letters all mixed up. In other words, if your name is Harvey Furd, you might write it as "Vreahy Urfd."

Put all of the names in a hat and have all the players draw pieces of paper. On "Go," have everyone try to unscramble the names on the pieces of paper they drew. They may figure them out by themselves or they can seek help from others. Once they know the names on their slips of paper, they must seek those people out—either by shouting out their names or by going around asking people their names. Once they find the right persons, they must have them sign their pieces of paper.

The game can be played with a time limit, or end when the names are all figured out.

Staff Stumpers

Here is a fun game that will really help kids get better acquainted with the staff (directors, sponsors, teachers). In advance of the game, have staff members answer a list of questions (with short answers) similar to these:

1. Why are you on staff?
2. What has been your most embarrassing moment while working with the group?

3. If you could go anywhere in the world, where would it be?
4. What makes you happy?
5. Who has had the most influence on your life?
6. Who is your favorite performer?
7. If you had a million dollars, what would you do with it?
8. My dream is to...(complete the sentence).
9. What is the best book that you have read recently (excluding the Bible)?
10. What is your favorite scripture verse?

After staff members fill out the questionnaire, print up their answers, along with the questions, in a multiple-choice type of quiz. For example, question number three might look like this:

3. If you could go anywhere in the world, where would it be?
   ___ 1. The French Riviera
   ___ 2. The Holy Land
   ___ 3. Home
   ___ 4. Butte, Montana
   ___ 5. Hawaii

The answers should be the actual answers given by staff members, and the object of the game is for the kids to try and guess which staff members gave which answers. The answers should be in a different order for each question.

After the kids have made their guesses, have the staff members come to the front and answer the questions correctly. The kids can then check their papers to see just how well they know their leaders.

Statistical Treasure Hunt

Here is an exceptionally good game for getting groups acquainted. Divide your group into teams of equal numbers, if possible. Give each team a typewritten or photocopied sheet of questions to answer and evaluate as indicated on their sheets. Each team needs to appoint a captain to act as the gleaner and recorder of information.

Below is a list of typical questions and scoring methods. You may not want to use all of these questions, or your staff may suggest other questions to you that may be more appropriate for your particular group or occasion.

General Questions:

_____ 1. Counting January as one point, February as two points, and so on through the calendar year, add up the total of birthday points at your table.

_____ 2. Counting one point for each different state named, give the score for the different number of birth states represented on your team.

_____ 3. Total of all shoe sizes added together (One foot only).

_____ 4. Total number of all baby teeth lost or adult teeth that have come in for everyone at your table.

_____ 5. Get your hair color score: Black counts two; brown counts one; blonde counts three; red counts five; gray counts three; white counts five.

_____ 6. Score a point for each self-made article worn or carried by your teammates.

_____ 7. Total the number of miles traveled by each member to get to this meeting.

_____ 8. Total the number of brothers and sisters that your teammates have.

_____ 9. Score one point for each different grade school attended.

Sticker Mixer

Here is a get-acquainted activity for larger groups. Write everyone's names on stickers (pressure-sensitive, round ones work best) and randomly distribute them. Have everyone stick the labels on their faces somewhere. The kids then try to find their own names on the faces of others. When they find their names, they get the stickers and put them on their shirts or coats and stay with the persons on whom they found their names until they find *their* names. This is a good way for kids to see a lot of faces in a short time.

Time-Bomb Ice Breaker

First, choose a volunteer to lead off this activity. The prop used in this mixer is a small, gift-wrapped box with a removable cover and a kitchen timer inside. These instructions appear on the cover:

"You have just been handed a time bomb. Hear it ticking? The only way you can get rid of it is to introduce yourself to a stranger in the room, tell that stranger where you are from and find out the person's name and where he or she is from. Then you may hand that person this gift."

The time you allow for introductions before the alarm goes off will vary depending on the size of the crowd, but the average is about five minutes. You can use more than one "bomb" for a larger crowd. When the alarm goes off, whoever is caught with the bomb is marked with a bandage on the forehead and seated in the middle of the room. These "victims" can be used later as "volunteers" for whichever activities in which you may need them. They will also be the ones to set or reset the alarms for shorter periods of time during which the introductions continue. This "gift giving" will go on until you have as many "volunteers" as you need for other events, or for about fifteen minutes, depending on the size of the group.

The "Us Quiz"

Give your group a quiz consisting of twenty-five questions like those below. The questions may vary from silly to serious. The person with the most correct answers wins a snapshot of the entire group. This is a good way to familiarize newcomers with your group and to remind the regulars of what the group is all about.

1. Name the event when we stayed overnight in a barn.
2. Who is our pastor?
3. Name two people in our group who are related.
4. What is the name of our church newsletter?
5. What refreshments were served last week?
6. Name two service projects that our group did last year.

Zip Zap

Zip Zap is a circle game designed for learning first names. The participants must find out who is seated to their left and to their right. Tell them, "The person on your left is your *Zip* and the person on your right is your *Zap*." Standing in the center of the circle, the leader points to different kids in turn and says: "Zip, one, two, three, four, five." When kids are pointed to, they must shout out the names of the people to their left (or Zip) before the leader reaches a count of of five. When the leader points to the different kids and says: "Zap, one, two, three, four, five," the kids pointed to must shout the names of the persons on their right. When a player pointed to fails, that player takes the leader's place in the center of the circle. The leader then takes the chair of the loser.

Crazy Crowd Breakers

These attention grabbers are intended as performances before audiences. They are designed for laughter and entertainment, not for humor at someone's expense. If the people chosen for these zany activities are "good sports" and the leader uses the activities skillfully, the results will be very positive and lots of fun.

Corn Shucking Race

For this game, you will need several ears of corn. Select three or more volunteers who will try to shuck an ear of corn using only their bare feet. No hands are allowed. Whoever finishes first, or whoever does the best job within a given time limit, is the winner. You can give a bag of corn chips to winners who then can share them with the rest of their groups.

Face Decorating

Have several couples participate in this one. Give one member of each pair the items necessary to decorate a cake (squeeze tubes of icing, whipped cream, candy sprinkles) and have them decorate their partners' faces. The decoratees should lie down on their backs during the decorating process. When

their faces are fully embellished, the decoratees stand and have their faces judged, either by the audience or a panel of judges.

Forty-Inch Dash

Give three or four kids thirty-inch pieces of string with marshmallows tied to one end. On a signal, the youngsters put the loose string ends in their mouths and, without using either of their hands, "eat" their way to the marshmallows. Your group will go wild watching the fun.

Obstacle Course

Challenge several kids or adults to walk blindfolded through an obstacle course of some kind. Choose volunteers who are good sports. Offer a fabulous prize to the individuals who can successfully navigate the course. Mark the course by scattering books, chairs, coats, buckets of water, and so on around the room. After the contestants have seen the course, send them out of the room. Bring them back in one at a time to walk the obstacle course. But while they are out, remove all the obstacles. It's really fun to watch as well as comic to do.

Rubber-Band Relay

Use three people in this "face coordination" test. Place rubber bands around the volunteers' heads, crossing over the tips of their noses. The idea is for a player to maneuver the rubber band from the nose down to the neck without using any hands. Any facial contortion is legal. The first participant to get the rub-ber band all the way down, or the participant who moves the rubber band the furthest wins.

Shoe the Donkey

This game can be played indoors or outdoors. You'll need two chairs, eight shoes, and two blindfolds. Two chairs are set up in the middle of the area. These are the donkeys. Then two kids are blindfolded and seated on the "donkeys." At least four kids donate their shoes and scatter them around the chairs. The object of the game is for the two players to locate and place shoes on each leg of their donkeys. The first one to shoe a donkey successfully is the winner.

To add excitement to the game, players may be allowed to steal the shoes already placed on each other's donkeys. This game guarantees squeals of laughter!

Snoot Shoot

The idea of this game is to see how far players can propel a bit of breakfast cereal across the room, using only the air from their noses! To play, mark out a line behind which players must stand. The players then place kernels in or near one nostril. While holding the other nostril shut with a finger, on the word "Fire," they must exhale through their noses with as much force as possi-

ble. Distance wins this game.

This is great as a crowd breaker, or as one event in a series of relays or target-shooting contests, with each team choosing a representative to compete.

Socks Up

Select two or three people and have them come to the front and sit in chairs, facing the audience. Have them take off their shoes. Give them each a pair of extra-large, knee-length athletic socks and a pair of garden gloves and blindfold them. Then have them race to put on their gloves and then their socks in the fastest time.

Tapehead

Whether you play this game as a relay or a watch-and-cheer game, it's hilarious! Young people wrap up their partner's heads completely with masking tape, sticky side out. (Do leave space for eyes, mouth, and nose.) Then, in competition, the partially mummified players crawl to an area where a variety of small, light, and safe-to-pick-up objects are spread out. They lower their heads onto objects, "stick" them with the masking tape, and bring them back to where their partners can remove the items and send them back for another load. The pair or team whose Tapehead fetches the most items in a given amount of time wins.

Here are some common articles easily picked up by a Tapehead: egg cartons, paper cups, construction paper, shoe boxes, milk cartons, paper clips, pie tins, rubber bands, cotton balls, aluminum foil, marshmallows, small stuffed animals, inflated balloons, and paper plates.

Tongue-Tie

This crowd breaker works well with older kids. Have three kids from your group come up to the front and give them each a piece of wrapped bubble gum. On a signal, the kids put the gum in their mouths, wrapper and all, and must then unwrap the gum without using their hands, spit out the wrapper, chew the gum, and blow a bubble. The first kid done wins.

Toothpaste Races

Give each team of two or three kids a new tube of toothpaste and a roll of toilet paper. The toilet paper is a "track" upon which to squeeze the toothpaste, so it's easy to clean up.

Race #1: Go for the longest unbroken strand of toothpaste in a set length of time.

Race #2: Lay out an "obstacle course" where the team must run the strand of toothpaste over all sorts of objects. If your group is really spirited, have some of the team members lie down and have other members run the toothpaste across their faces.

Race #3: Go for the longest single strand from one new tube of paste per team, this time without a time limit.

Un-Banana

Ask the adult volunteer sponsors or parents to come up in front of the group. Have them race to see who can peel a banana, eat it, and then drink a can of ginger ale the fastest. Watch their mouths foam up. Give the winner a bunch of bananas and a six-pack of soft drinks.

Whistle and Burp

For this game, select two or three girls and two or three boys per team. The boys each get five saltine crackers and the girls each get a bottle of cola. On a signal, the boys must eat the crackers and whistle and the girls must drink the cola and burp. The gender to finish first wins.

Group Engagers

The attention grabbers found here involve all of your group members. They are designed to produce both laughter and interaction. Use them as crowd breakers and meeting starters when you want group participation.

Baby-Picture Guess

This is a great idea that helps your kids see the human sides of their adult leaders. Obtain baby pictures of all your adult leaders. Pass around each of the pictures, one at a time. The kids are all given pieces of paper and pencils and try to guess the identity of each baby as the pictures are passed around. If you have a large group of kids you will need to make slides of the snapshots so that they can be displayed using a slide projector.

Instead of (or in addition to) baby pictures, you can use pictures of your adult leaders when they were in elementary school.

Bible Family Feud

Survey your adult Sunday-school class members to get their answers to ques- tions like the ones listed below. On the surveys, people are asked to give one answer per question. Then compile your "survey results," rank-ordering all the answers from most to least common, and use these results in a game of "Family Feud," patterned after the popular TV show. It's easiest if you play for games rather than points, like they do on TV. Each team sends a player to the front. A question is asked of these two players. The player giving the most common response has the option of playing the game or passing it to the player from the other team. The team that plays the game must name all the responses given (or a maximum of the top six responses) without making three mistakes. If it does, it is the winning team. If not, the other team has a chance to "steal" the game if it can name a correct response not named by the other team. The team winning the most games, or the best two out of three, is the winner. Possible Questions:

1. Name a disciple of Jesus.
2. Name one of the Ten Commandments.
3. Name a parable of Jesus.
4. Name a city in Israel.
5. Name a miracle of Jesus.
6. Name one of the fruits of the Spirit.
7. Name one of Paul's letters.
8. Name one of the plagues of Egypt.
9. Name a famous Old Testament character.
10. Name a famous New Testament character.

Chocolate Bar Scramble

This game is best used with groups of six to twelve players. If you have more, divide into two or more groups and get several games going at once. To play, you will need wrapped chocolate candy bars, hats, scarves, pairs of gloves, knives and forks, and dice (use either one die per group or a pair of dice if you wish to make the game tougher than it already is).

The groups form circles and place everything except the dice on tables somewhere near their circles. The dice are then passed around the circles and all of the players are given turns rolling them. When players roll sixes (if you are playing with a pair of dice, the rolls are either twos or sevens), they rush to the table, put on hats, scarves, and gloves, and use the knives and forks to unwrap and eat the candy bars, one slice at a time. If you keep the slices relatively

small, the games will last longer. Players must swallow their slices before they cut

more from the candy bars. While players attempt to eat the candy bars, the dice are still going around the circle as quickly as possible, with each of the participants attempting to roll sixes. As soon as another six is rolled, the person who rolled it takes a turn at the table, putting on the hat, scarf, and gloves and attacking the chocolate bar with a knife and fork (preferably clean).

When another six is rolled, the player at that group's table removes whatever was put on (hat, scarf or gloves) and returns to the circle, even if none of the candy bar was eaten. It's important to remember that any player making it to the table must put on the hat, scarf, and gloves before getting to eat any of the candy. Of course, many players who get to the table will not get any chocolate bar, as their turns will be over before they get that far.

The game is over when the candy bar is devoured, or when everyone drops to the floor with exhaustion. More candy bars can be added to extend play.

Folding Up

Provide all kinds of pieces of paper, square or rectangular. Have at least one for each kid. Include napkins, notebook paper, tissue paper, newspaper, construction paper, toilet paper, and paper towels. Make sure there are a few extra-large pieces. The kids are all instructed to choose pieces before they are told what the papers are for.

Offer five-dollar bills to any contestants who can fold their pieces of paper in half nine times or more (eight is the absolute limit). Try it yourself first!

Grab a Guess

Give each person a pencil and a sheet of paper numbered one through thirty. Have someone stand behind a blanket hung up to form a curtain, holding a bag that contains the items listed below. That person will take one item out at a time and allow the rest of the group to take turns (five seconds only) touching the object with their hands. No one, however, is allowed to see the items behind the curtain. After an object is touched, players return to their seats and write down what they think the object is. The aim of the game is to see how many correct guesses the players can make.

1. eraser	11. stuffed animal	21. TV remote control
2. dime	12. guitar pick	22. computer floppy disk
3. key	13. comb	23. extension cord
4. paper cup	14. envelope	24. flashlight battery
5. coffee stirrer	15. rubber band	25. clock or watch
6. pen	16. Band-Aid	26. toy car
7. cassette tape	17. spool of thread	27. cotton ball
8. crayon	18. postage stamp	28. empty soda can
9. paper clip	19. chalk	29. a jack from a jack set
10. spoon	20. calculator	30. candle

Guess What?

Here's a good game that can be used as a crowd breaker at the beginning of an event while people are still arriving. You will need to do a little advance preparation by placing various items around the room: a jar full of small balls or beans, a ribbon hanging from the ceiling, a display of photos of famous (or not so famous) people, a package that you have weighed in advance, a box with something in it, and an assortment of bottles, each containing a different substance that gives off an odor. Then give each person a game sheet like the one on the following page.

When everyone has had enough time to try to figure out the answers, announce the correct answers and award a prize to whoever gets the most answers correct, or award separate prizes to the winners in each of the various categories.

Human Scavenger Hunt

Divide into teams and have each team choose a leader. All team members must stay within a designated area. A "judge" stands in a position that is an equal distance from all the teams. For example, if there are four teams, then the teams can position themselves in the four corners of the room and the "judge" can stand in the middle.

The "judge" calls out a characteristic similar to the ones below and the leaders on each team try to locate someone on their teams that fit the characteristic. As soon as someone is found, the leader sends that person to the judge. The first team to have a person reach the judge wins.

Here are some sample characteristics: Someone who . . .

1. Has blue eyes and brown hair.
2. Received all A's in the last marking period.
3. Ate at MacDonald's today.
4. Took a vitamin today.
5. Watched TV cartoons last Saturday.
6. Likes broccoli.
7. Said "Hi" to someone today.
8. Memorized a Bible verse this week.
9. Is wearing Nike sneakers.
10. Is chewing green gum.
11. Has never had a cavity.
12. Owns a dog.
13. Did not eat breakfast this morning.
14. Visited a foreign country this past year.
15. Likes arithmetic.

Human Scrabble

Divide the group into teams. Randomly distribute cards that have letters of the alphabet written on them. On a signal, each team must use the letters they were dealt to form the longest words that they possibly can. The longest word

COUNT! MEASURE! LIFT! SNIFF!

Number 1

How many balls are in the JAR?

_____

Number 2

How many inches long is the RIBBON? _____ inches

Number 3

Write the names of the people in the PICTURES.

1. _____

2. _____

3. _____

4. _____

5. _____

Number 4

How much does the PACKAGE weigh? _____ lbs. _____ oz.

Number 5

What is the substance in each of the BOTTLES?

1. _____

2. _____

3. _____

4. _____

5. _____

Keep this paper. The _correct answers_ will be announced.

wins. Mix all the letter cards up again, redistribute them, and play several rounds. Each round lasts thirty seconds. Be sure to include plenty of common letters, especially vowels.

For a variation of this game, see "Crossword People" on page 106.

Letter Scramble

Before your next meeting, tape letters of the alphabet to the bottoms of all the chairs in the room. When the kids sit down have them get their letters. Call out a word, and the first group of kids that can form the word—holding up its letters and standing in order before the group—gets a prize.

Mad Ads

Divide your group into teams of two or three persons and give each team a magazine (the same one for every team). Teams should appoint a "runner." The leader then calls out a description of an ad somewhere in the magazine. The first team to tear out the ad from the magazine, give it to the runner, and have the runner get it to the leader, wins. You also can call out descriptions of photos, titles of articles, and so on.

Name That Video

Video-arcade dwellers will shine at this game, which requires kids to identify video games by their sounds. It takes about a half an hour of preparation time. Take a portable tape recorder to your local video arcade and get the manager's permission to record the characteristic tunes and sounds of twenty or so games.

With the recorder on, preface each game's sounds with a spoken number; for example, "This is game number one." Then place the microphone near the speakers to capture that game's distinctive audio effects. After you get thirty seconds to a minute or so of sounds, turn off the recorder and write down the number and the game's name for your own reference. Then on to another game.

You don't have to spend a roll of quarters to do this, either. Some games emit a continual patter to attract players; take advantage of these. Or you can ask players if you can record while they play.

With your cassette of electronic sounds in hand, go to your meeting or social event, let your video-game experts be captains, choose teams, and give the teams sheets of paper and pencils. Separate the teams from each other and announce the rules: as you play the mystery sounds, the teams must quietly discuss the possibilities, arrive at a consensus, and record their decision on paper. Following the playing of all the sounds, correct names are given; the team with the most correct answers wins.

The prize? Tokens from the local arcade!

Newspaper Costumes

Divide the kids up so that there are three in each group. Give each group twelve sheets of newspaper and eight pieces of masking tape. The contest is to see which group can make the most original costume, neatness counting, of course. Have a judge choose the winning group.

Observation Game

Send someone out of the room. While that person is gone, ask the others to list things they remember about the person's appearance. For example, does the person wear glasses? What kind and color of shoes, pants, and shirt does the person have on? Write the observations down on a blackboard and have the individual come back into the room. Compare reality with the descriptions. Follow up with a discussion on how much we notice about others. It might be a good idea to "fix" the person up ahead of time—that is, give the individual some distinct things to wear, like a leather watchband, a pencil behind the ear, monogrammed shirt, and so on.

Revolving Story

Begin at one side of the room or circle. The first person begins to make up a fairy tale of some kind. This person continues for ten seconds and at a signal the next person in line adds to the story for ten seconds and so on down the line. The results are usually quite funny.

Stick It

Here's a game of skill that can be played by as few as two people. You'll need the following items: two light ropes or cords about ten feet long, several dowels (round sticks) about twelve inches long, a box big enough for the dowels to fit inside, a chair, and a lectern or something similar.

Tack the two cords to the lectern two inches apart and stretch the ropes back to the chair, ten feet away. One person stands on the chair and holds the ropes. The box is placed approximately two-thirds of the way from the chair under the ropes. A second player places the dowels (one at a time) on the two ropes

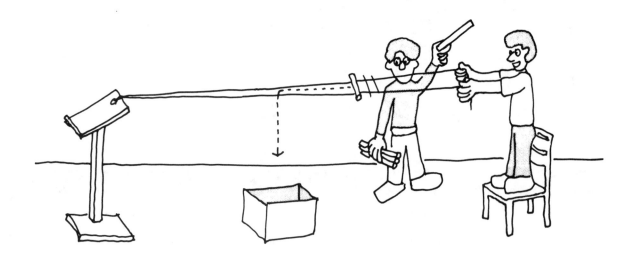

at the holder's hands, and the holder tries to roll the dowel down the ropes and into the box. If the holder fails she or he must try again. Players can be timed (best time to get them all in wins) or two can go at the same time for a good race. For team relays, each person gets a dowel, and each must get all the dowels in the box.

Sucker Relay

Teams line up. Give each person a paper straw. They must pick up a piece of paper (about four inches square) by sucking on the straw and carry it around a goal and back. If the paper is dropped, the player must start over. Each person on the team must participate and the first team to finish wins.

Team Crossword

Here's a good group engager that requires some quick thinking. Get a book of crossword puzzles and select one that would be about the right difficulty for your group. Reproduce the crossword puzzle on a large piece of butcher paper, or project it on the wall with an overhead projector. Divide your group into two or more teams. After you read the clue, the first team to shout out the right answer gets fifty points for every blank letter space it can fill.

The team with the correct answer then gets to select which clue is read next, and so forth. It's usually a good idea to have one person read the clues, and another person fill in the correct responses and keep score. If one team gets too far ahead, give triple-point value on the last few words and give the teams that are behind a chance to catch up.

Used Attention Grabbers

To get double duty out of many of the attention grabbers found in this book, have someone videotape them as they take place. Then show them a few weeks later and your group will find they are just as funny to watch as they were to play.

Skits That Grab

Try one of these hilarious skits at your next retreat, camp, or group meeting. Skits are great introductory activities that create a fun, casual atmosphere.

This skit can be done in one of two ways. Either divide your entire group into ten small groups, or have ten individual kids come to the front of the room. The narrator reads the following story and as the names listed below are mentioned, whoever is assigned those names (one person or small group) yells out the proper sound effects. At the end of the story when the reader says, "Ride 'em Cowboy!" the entire group is told to jump up and do their parts en masse.

The Characters:

Rattlesnakes—hiss rattle, rattle, hiss rattle, rattle

Cowboys—yippee
Bessie—screams or wails
Love—coo-o-o-o
Bandits—grr-r-r-r
Horses—stamp feet
Cattle—moo-o-o-o
Guns—bang, bang
Wolves—yow-o-o-o
Villain—ah-h-h-h-h-h-h-h-hah-h-h-h

The Story:

There once was a handsome cowboy ... named Bill Jones, who lived far, far out west on a great ranch. He spent most of his days riding the range on a fine black horse ... named Napoleon, and following his herds of bawling white-faced cattle . . .

On an adjoining ranch lived beautiful Bessie . . . Brown with her aged parents. All the cowboys . . . loved Bessie . . . but especially did the heart of the handsome Bill go pitter-patter when he looked into her eyes, which were limpid pools of darkness. The bold bandit . . . Two-Gun Sam also did feign to win the heart of beautiful Bessie . . . but she spurned his love . . .

One day Bessie's father and mother received a letter asking them to come to town at once for the bad villain . . . was about to foreclose on the mortgage to their ranch. Mr. Brown hitched up the horses . . . they put their guns . . . in the wagon, and Mrs. Brown placed her rattlesnake . . . charm in her purse, and they drove away to town.

"Ahh—Haa!" cried the bold bandit . . . Two-Gun Sam, when they were out of sight; for he had forged the letter. "Now, I shall have the love . . . of the Beautiful Bessie . . ." So he rode his horse . . . up to the house, shot both of his guns . . . Beautiful Bessie . . . ran out of the house to see if someone had killed a wolf . . . or a rattlesnake . . . When the girl saw Two-Gun Sam, she started to run for her horse . . . But the bold bandit . . . grabbed her by the wrist. "Ah, proud beauty," said he. "You shall be my wife and someday I shall own all of your father's cattle . . ."

"Never," said Bessie . . . "I do not love . . . you."

"Then perhaps, you would rather be taken to a den of rattlesnakes . . . or eaten by the wolves . . . or trampled by the cattle . . . ?"

"Ah, yes, anything rather than let you steal my love . . . and take my father's cattle . . . Unhand me, you villain . . . "

"Very well, proud beauty, to the rattlesnakes . . . we go." And he put her on a horse . . . and started to speed away.

Gun . . . shots rang out, and the two bullets went through the top of the bold bandit's . . . sombrero. "Stop, villain . . . !, rattlesnake . . . wolf . . . !" It was the handsome cowboy . . . Bill Jones.

When Two-Gun Sam saw the cowboy . . . he muttered to himself, "Curses, foiled again." He dropped Beautiful Bessie . . . from his horse . . . threw his gun . . . away and started for the hills where the wolves . . . and rattlesnakes . . . and cattle . . . roam, for he knew he would never win the love . . . of Bessie . . . nor get her father's cattle . . .

The handsome cowboy . . . looked into the eyes of the beautiful Bessie . . . which were still limpid pools of darkness, and they both forgot about the wolves . . . and the rattlesnakes . . . and the villain . . . who wanted Mr. Brown's cattle . . .

Bessie . . . thanked the handsome cowboy for rescuing her from the bold bandit . . . and she told Bill that she had been saving her love . . . for him. So they rode off together on their horses . . .

RIDE 'EM COWBOY!

Creative Theme Skits

Here's a fun idea for retreats or meetings that involves total participation. Put several ordinary objects in as many sacks as you have teams. Objects should be things like paper clips, cotton swabs, and popsicle sticks. Put the same things in each sack and give each team twenty minutes to form a skit around a selected theme. The skit can be serious or funny but each team must use every item in the sack and every team member must be involved.

After the time limit is up, have each team present its skit.

The Enlarging Machine

For this skit you need a large refrigerator box with a hole in it, and dials, knobs, and meters painted on it like a computer. Inside the box, concealed from the audience is a secret helper.

The creator of the machine, Dr. Cowdungski, demonstrates. He throws a handkerchief into the hole and out comes a sheet; a piece of string comes out as a rope; a ping-pong ball comes out a basketball. Applause follows each demonstration. A lady then walks by, carrying a doll. Just as she gets in front of the machine, she trips and accidentally tosses the "baby" into the machine. The scientist yells, "Oh, no!" and out of the machine bursts the "helper," a big guy in diapers with a bottle, shouting, "MOMMY!"

Fun With Emcees

An often neglected part of a skit night or talent show is the art of emceeing. Instead of being traditional and using one emcee, why not try using two? Here are a few possibilities:

1. *Stereo Emcees:* The cohosts each can give phrases of the introduction, with both of them saying the last phrase simultaneously.
   Cohost One: The next skit . . .
   Cohost Two: we would like to . . .
   Cohost One: present to you . . .
   Both cohosts: is entitled "The Stuntman."

2. *Bobbing Emcees:* One cohost stands behind the other. The introduction is broken down word by word. The front cohost says the first word, squats down, and the second cohost stands and says the second word. This con-

tinues until the introduction is finished.

3. *Echoing Emcees:* Each cohost has a microphone. One cohost gives the introduction, while the other echoes.

4. *Singing Emcees:* Both cohosts can sing the introduction to their own made-up tune or to the tune of a popular song or commercial jingle.

5. *Ventriloquist and Dummy:* One cohost is the ventriloquist, while the other is the dummy. The dummy sits on the ventriloquist's lap while the ventriloquist tells a few jokes and then announces the skit.

Hey, Dumbrowsky

A battle is in progress. Behind one barricade are four soldiers shooting at four soldiers behind another barricade, a few feet away. One army has a red flag and the other a blue flag. As the fighting progresses, one of the blue soldiers yells to the red army: "Hey, Finkbeiner!" Finkbeiner, one of the red soldiers, stands up (unprotected) and says, "Yeah, what do you want?" The blue army then shoots Finkbeiner and he falls. One of the blue soldiers then yells, "Hey, Klutzenberg!" Klutzenberg, another red soldier, stands up and says, "Yes, did you call me?" He gets shot also. Again, the blue army calls out another name, "Hey Farnsworthy!" Farnsworthy stands up, answers, and gets shot like the others. Now, only Dumbrowsky is left in the red army. He scratches his head and says, "Ah-ha! I get it! They call out our names, we stand up, and then they shoot us. Well, we can play that little game too!" So Dumbrowsky yells out: "Hey, Smith!" Smith (one of the blue soldiers) does not stand up, but yells back, "Hey, is that you Dumbrowsky?" Dumbrowsky then stands up and says, "Yeah, it's me!" Dumbrowsky then gets shot.

Howdy, Buckaroo!

If the kids in your group have a tough time memorizing lines, this skit may be perfect for them. Four characters are needed: a "mechanical" quick-draw cowboy dressed in full Old West garb, two warehouse employees dressed appropriately, and a third employee. The only props you will need are two gun-and-holster sets, one of which should be loaded with blanks. Only the mechanical quick-draw cowboy needs to remember any lines. They should be spoken in a mechanical manner: "Howdy Buckaroo. So you think you can beat me, eh? Put on the holster at my feet and on the count of three, draw! Are you ready? One . . . . Two . . . . Three!"

The play begins with the first two warehouse employees rolling in the mechanical slot-machine cowboy for storage. The extra gun-and-holster set is placed at the feet of the mechanical cowboy.

The third employee walks in and, seeing the robot, decides to try his luck. He reads the instructions printed on the chest of the mechanical man and then places a quarter in the slot. The robot winds up and gives the memorized speech. The employee is unable to pick up the extra gun-and-holster set because it is trapped under the boot of the mechanical cowboy. He panics and turns to run as the robot counts to three and shoots one of the first two employees.

Not to be outdone, the third employee lifts the robot's leg and puts on the gun set before inserting another quarter. He even practices his quick-draw skills several times. Feeling quite secure, he inserts another quarter. The message is repeated, but this time his gun sticks in the holster and the other of the first two employees is shot also.

For the final attempt, the third employee pulls his gun, stands to the side, and holds his gun to the robot's head as he inserts another quarter. The robot repeats the message except this time the mechanical cowboy winds down in the middle of "two." The employee bangs on the robot a couple of times to get him moving again, but there's no response. Disgusted, he takes off the gun, sets it down at the robot's feet, and turns to walk off. The robot suddenly jerks to life with the rest of the prerecorded message, and says "three," shooting the third employee.

Monk Monotony

The following skit is an easy one to pull off. There are three characters: the Main Monk, Monk Monotony, and a sign carrier. And there is only one prop: a large sign that reads, "Ten Years Later." The audience is asked to imagine the monastery where Monk Monotony has just taken a vow of silence.

Main Monk: So, Monk Monotony, you have just taken a vow of silence? *(Monk Monotony shakes head "yes")* Do you know what this vow of silence means? *(Monk Monotony shakes head "yes")* That's right, you can only say two words for the next ten years. You may go now. *(Monk Monotony exits. After about twenty seconds in which the Main Monk does nothing, the sign carrier enters slowly from right and exits slowly to the left, carrying the sign that reads, "Ten Years Later." Monk Monotony enters)*

Main Monk: Yes, Monk Monotony, your first ten years are up, and you may now say your two words.

Monk Monotony: Hard bed.

Main Monk: You may go now. *(Monk Monotony exits. After about twenty seconds in which the Main Monk does nothing, the sign carrier enters slowly from right and exits slowly*

	to the left, carrying the sign that reads, "Ten Years Later." Monk Monotony enters)
Main Monk:	Yes, Monk Monotony, your second ten years are up, and you may now say your two words.
Monk Monotony:	Bad food.
Main Monk:	You may go now. *(Monk Monotony exits. After about twenty seconds in which the Main Monk does nothing, the sign carrier enters slowly from the right and exits slowly to the left, carrying the sign that reads, "Ten Years Later." Monk Monotony enters)*
Main Monk:	Yes, Monk Monotony, your third ten years are up, and you may now say your two words.
Monk Monotony:	I quit. *(He turns to exit.)*
Main Monk:	*(To Monk Monotony, as he is leaving)* Well, I am not surprised! You've been complaining ever since you got here.

The Seagull and the Surfer

Here is a great spontaneous skit that demands no props or preparation. The actors can be chosen on the spot. Their instructions are simple. As the narrator reads the story slowly, each character acts out what is being described. For example: "The waves rise in great swells" *(the people who are waves begin to rise up and down)*. Be sure the narrator gives the actors enough time to do what is being described.

Characters:
Sun
Seagulls (any number)
Waves (any number)
Surfer
Shore (any number)

Narrator:
It is a bright and beautiful morning at the beach. The sun is slowly rising, and the seagulls are waking up after a long night's rest. The waves are calm and serene and the shore is smooth and damp.

The ocean world seems to come alive as the seagulls chatter to each other and fly off on their morning search for food. As the gulls are flying over the shore and waves, they begin to get playful. They soar higher and higher, then drop suddenly, skimming the waves with their outstretched wings. They fly up, then down, then up and down again, in circles, in zigzags, backward, then forward. The gulls are chattering noisily, screaming as loudly as they can. Gradually, the playfulness ends, and the gulls return slowly to their nests to rest.

The waves are beginning to rise in great swells. They rise higher and higher, reaching farther and farther until, at the last second, they come crashing down on each other and roll on to the shore.

A surfer arrives at the beach, and steps on the shore. Excited at the prospect of the big waves that are continuing to break on the shore, the surfer begins to jump up and down. He sits on the edge of the shore and gazes at the breaking waves.

The surfer now decides to take his "surfboard" out into the water. He paddles out, making fast, long strokes. He paddles faster and faster, with longer and harder strokes, until he reaches the point where he is past the waves. He uses his skill to dodge in and out of the waves with precision timing. He is full of poise and grace as he "hangs ten" on his surfboard. Then suddenly a wave grabs him and sends him crashing into the shore.

The surfer, now tired and beaten, gathers up his surfboard and slowly stumbles away from the shore, heading for home.

The day is coming to an end as the sun slowly sets. The birds make their last flight for the day, flying over the shore and waves, and once again returning to their nests for a cozy night's sleep, tucking their wings under their bodies and lowering their heads.

As we take one last look at the beautiful ocean scene before the sun sets, we can see the restful seagulls and the waves beating on the shore.

Spontaneous Melodrama

This skit requires no preparation, except for collecting a few appropriate costumes. It works best with larger groups, and may be used with any age group. It requires nine participants plus a narrator, who are chosen right out of the audience. They have no lines to read or to memorize. All they have to do is act out the story as it is read by the narrator. When you select volunteers, try to choose people who are uninhibited and willing to give the skit their best shot. Also try to match the right kinds of personalities with the parts required.

Characters Needed:
The Hero, Dudley Do Right
The Heroine, Prudence Pureheart
The Villain, Dirty Dan
The Grandmother
The Dog (a boy who gets down on all fours)
The Cat (a girl who does the same)
The Chair (someone else on their hands and knees)

The Table (two people, side by side on all fours)

After the characters are chosen from the audience, have an assistant take them all backstage and dress them up in the costumes described below.

Costume suggestions:
Be creative! The more ridiculous, the better.
Dudley: White boots and a Mickey Mouse hat
Prudence: Long blonde wig and a skirt
Villain: Black cape, mustache, and a top hat
Grandmother: Gray wig, shawl, and glasses

As soon as the actors are ready, the narrator begins reading the script. The audience is instructed to *boo* the villain, *cheer* for the hero, and so on. The narrator should read the script with feeling and pause in the appropriate places, allowing time for the actors to act and the audience to react. To give them more incentive to act with gusto, you might inform the performers that the audience will vote for best actor at the conclusion.

The narrator reads the following script:

As our story opens, we find ourselves in a densely wooded forest where lovely PRUDENCE PUREHEART is picking wild blackberries and whistling a merry tune. (Pause while Prudence whistles) Unbeknownst to her, the village villain, DIRTY DAN, is creeping up behind her.

He grabs her and tries to steal a kiss!

She screams loud and long.

The villain covers her mouth with his hand as she screams.

She slaps the villain in the face.

He picks her up, throws her over his shoulder, and carries her.

She screams and beats him.

He marches around in a circle three times, then heads off to steal her Grandmother's money.

They exit.

MEANWHILE . . .

Back at the ranch, Prudence's GRANDMOTHER is sitting on a CHAIR, stirring some cake batter over the TABLE.

The CAT is sleeping underneath the table.

The old DOG, Shep, enters the house and barks at the cat.

The cat jumps into Grandma's lap.

Grandmother slaps the cat and says, "Get down, you dirty creature."

The cat jumps down and runs outside.

The dog comes over and licks Grandma's hand.

He keeps licking her hand all the way up to the elbow.

Grandma kicks the dog.

The dog goes and lies in the corner.

Just then, the villain enters the room with Prudence over his shoulder.

Grandmother screams.

The villain says, "I am taking Prudence and your money."

The dog rushes over and bites the villain on the leg.

The villain kicks the dog and puts down Prudence.

Prudence faints onto the floor.

The dog barks at the villain, then goes over and starts licking Prudence's face to revive her.

He licks her face for fifteen seconds, while she remains perfectly still.

Just then, our hero, DUDLEY DO RIGHT, enters and shouts, "Forsooth and anon!"

Prudence stands up and screams, "Oh, my darling Dudley!"

Dudley and Prudence embrace.

Dudley says, "I love you, my precious."

Prudence says, "I love you, my lotus blossom."

All of a sudden, the villain grabs the chair and throws it at Dudley.

It knocks Dudley down to the floor.

Prudence faints and falls onto the table.

Grandmother tries to revive her by slapping her hand, while sobbing, "My child, my child." This goes on and on.

The cat reenters the house, jumps on the chair, and then runs underneath the table.

Dudley stands up and begins flexing his muscles.

The villain begins to tremble and shake and his knees knock together. This goes on and on. The dog starts barking and the cat starts meowing, and this goes on and on.

Dudley decides to warm up for the fight so he does a few exercises, starting with ten jumping jacks. Then he runs in place for fifteen seconds.

All this while Grandmother is sobbing and slapping, the villain is trembling, the dog is barking, and the cat is meowing.

Then Dudley does fifteen pushups. On the fifteenth pushup, the villain seizes his opportunity and hits Dudley on the head.

Dudley falls to the floor, unconscious.

Just then, the cat scratches the dog's nose.

The dog and cat have a fight right over Dudley for ten seconds.

Then the dog chases the cat outside. Just then, the table collapses under Prudence's weight and falls to the ground, table, Prudence, Grandmother, and all.

Prudence remains unconscious.

Granny shouts, "You nasty villain!" and starts hitting Dirty Dan in the stomach.

The villain doubles over.

Granny then goes around and kicks him in the seat.

Dirty Dan straightens up.

Granny hits him some more in the stomach, over and over.

The villain again bends over.

She gives him a rabbit punch on the back of the neck.

He collapses unconscious to the floor.

Granny looks around at the three unconscious bodies.

She then straightens her shawl, adjusts her wig, and heads for the door to spend a night on the town, saying, "All's well that ends well!"

Music Madness

For some unusual ways to use music to grab your group's attention, try out one of these activities.

Marching Kazoo Band

This is another great activity for your entire group. Give every kid a kazoo and a marching band "uniform" (party hats work fine). Have your group come up with some wild marching drills and formations. As they perform, have recorded marches playing in the background, such as "Stars and Stripes Forever," to add some quality to the music and to help the band stay in beat.

Musical Showdown

This activity is great for total-group involvement. Divide the group into several different teams, each with a captain. Each group should have a name or a number to identify itself. Give each team a pencil and paper and several minutes to think of some songs they all know. They should be able to come up with five to ten songs.

Now it's time for the showdown. The leader shouts out the name of a group, and within five seconds the group must start singing a song. Then, at any point in the song, the leader blows a whistle and shouts out the name of another group. That group must start singing a different song within five seconds. (To add excitement and a little confusion to the game, the leader can shout out the name of the group that is already singing.) This continues, with the leader calling upon each group until all but one are eliminated.

Groups are disqualified if they sing a song that has already been sung, don't start a new song within five seconds, or if less than half their group is singing the song. Groups may add songs to their lists during the showdown. To narrow things down, you might choose a particular theme for the songs, like Christmas, hymns, or preschool songs. It's a lot of fun.

Recycled Hymns

Have group members go through your church hymnal and choose their favorite hymns. Then spend a meeting or two rewriting the words. Photocopy the best ones and sing them at your meetings or with the adults in the main service. These recycled hymns might become so well liked that they become a regular part of your worship.

Singing Circles

If your group likes to sing, this game will be an instant winner. If your group doesn't like to sing, then maybe this crowd breaker will cure them. Here's how it works. Divide into small groups of about five or six. If your group is already quite small, then just divide into two teams. In advance, think up a number of common words like:

Jesus	Peace	Prayer
Abide	Fellowship	Love
Comfort	Glory	King

These words can be written on cards, or you can just write them on the blackboard when you are ready for them. Choose some easy words and a few that are not so easy.

The game can be played several different ways. One way is to hold up one of the words and have each group try to be first to stand and sing a song that has that word in it. Another way to play is to give each group a stack of cards with all the words. The groups then get five minutes to get organized and come up with the songs they want to sing. Again, the idea is to sing a different song for each word. Then, each team stands and sings its songs, holding up the appropriate word for that song.

Judges determine the winner. This game can be used with secular hymns as well as with hymns and gospel choruses.

The Twelve Days of School

Here's a fun song that the group can sing, or you can use it as a skit with a different person taking each line and acting out each part. It should be sung to the same tune as "The Twelve Days of Christmas."

"On the first day of school, my mommy said to me . . . "

First day: "Don't ever wet your pants."
Second day: "Don't lift your dress."
Third day: "Don't eat your crayons."
Fourth day: "Don't chew gum."
Fifth day: "Don't pick your nose."
Sixth day: "Don't hold hands."
Seventh day: "Don't throw spitballs."
Eighth day: "Don't ever belch."
Ninth day: "Don't sleep in class."
Tenth day: "Don't be a sissy."
Eleventh day: "Don't bite your toenails."
Twelfth day: "Don't kiss the girls (boys)."

Up and Down Bonnie

Here's a fun variation to the song, "My Bonnie Lies Over the Ocean." While singing the song, have everyone stand on the first word that begins with a "B" and sit down on the next word that begins with "B." Continue the same process on all the "B" words. For another variation, have half the group start the song standing up. People get confused about whether they are to be standing or sitting. This will generate lots of laughs and is great to do with parents.

Servant Events

Older elementary-age kids can be and *need* to be involved in service projects. Here are a few creative ideas for engaging your group in mission and Christian service.

Admission for Missions

To help collect needed supplies for a mission hospital that is supported by your church or denomination, charge "admission" to one of your special events. Have each kid attending bring one of the following items to get in:

Aspirin—baby and adult
Multivitamins—with or without iron
Iron pills
Antibiotic ointments
Adhesive tape
White cotton thread
Sturdy paper cups and used margarine tubs
Containers for the children's ward
Hand soap
Instant soup
Baby cereal
Scrub brushes
Sanitary napkins
Hand towels
Sheets
Blankets

Adjust the list to fit your own mission hospital's needs.

Adopt-a-Garden

Here's an idea that can really "grow" on your group: Invite members to adopt the gardens of shut-ins, chronically ill, hospitalized, or aged people. Create youth/adult partnerships with three to four young people and one or two adults per group. Supply the seeds and encourage the teams to round up tools and lend the muscle power. They can prepare the soil, plant, cultivate, and ultimately harvest the crops of vegetables, all for the people who own the gardens, and who, of course, are unable to do the work. It makes for great interaction between the generations!

An adaptation of this idea involves others in the congregation. While publicizing "Adopt-a-Garden," invite others who already have gardens to set aside one or two rows for food to donate to the hungry. Again, your group can supply the seeds, and after the harvest, each team of young people and adults can deliver the food to the needy. This can fit well into a long-range, hunger-awareness program.

Bread-Baking Bash

Collect the ingredients needed to bake up plenty of bread, both loaves and rolls. With a good number of adult helpers, conduct a morning of bread baking (a Saturday usually works best): prepare the dough, get it into pans, and then let it rise. While it's rising, the kids can play some games and generally just have a good time until the bread is baked.

When the bread is finished, prepare some soup and have a lunch featuring hot soup and freshly baked bread. After lunch, wrap the other loaves (there should be more than the kids can eat) and visit the homes of some elderly members of the church. Spend a short time visiting with them and leave them with homemade loaves of bread, along with notes of appreciation, like, "Thanks for being a part of our church family." They'll love the thoughtfulness exhibited, and the obvious time sacrificed will help build relationships between the young and the old. You could conclude the day with a discussion of what happened while visiting the elderly, and perhaps a Bible lesson relating to "bread."

Can Hunt

Divide your group into teams that have a mix of adults and kids, and send them into the neighborhood for a limited time (thirty to forty-five minutes) to collect canned goods. The group with the most cans collected within the time limit wins a prize. It's amazing how many canned goods your group can collect if they are motivated by a contest. For some reason, people respond better when they can help someone win a contest than they do when they are simply helping a hungry family. The canned goods can be donated to your field mission or to a local food bank.

Flies, Gnats, and Mosquitoes

Once your kids are assembled in a circle, select a Safety Guard and a player to be "It." All the other players in the circle then count off as Flies, Gnats, or Mosquitoes. There should be equal numbers in each group of flying pests. "It" is blindfolded with a blindfold and is led to the the middle of the circle. "It" is spun around three times and given a fly swatter made out of a loosely rolled news-

paper or magazine. "It" is then bothered by the flying pests and must attempt to swat them. The Safety Guard monitors the swatting so that it does not become hitting. "It" calls out one or more of the pest names and begins to swat at them below the waist. When a category is called (Flies, Gnats, or Mosquitoes), all the players in that group must move to new positions in the circle. They can tiptoe, crawl, or quietly walk to change seats—whichever is the sneakiest so they can avoid being swatted—but they must stay inside the circle. The first moving player to be swatted becomes the new "It." If no one changing positions is swatted, the Safety Guard calls out, "The air is clear," and "It" knows to call out another pest name and try again.

The pests can bother "It," buzzing close by, but they risk a greater chance of getting swatted. "It" also can call out "Fly Swatter," and *all* the kids in the circle have to change seats, increasing the chances that "It" will be able to swat another player.

Gleaning Party

If your community has public garden plots or is in an area where there are many farms, your group might consider the old custom of gleaning—going through the fields after the harvest and salvaging what is ripe and usable. Sort the collected food and then give it to your local food bank or another organization that distributes food to the hungry.

Goof Checks and Thanks Checks

Photocopy a stack of the blank checks shown below and give them to your kids. Explain to the group that they can be used with their families as a clever way to say thanks, show love, or apologize for a goof up of some kind.

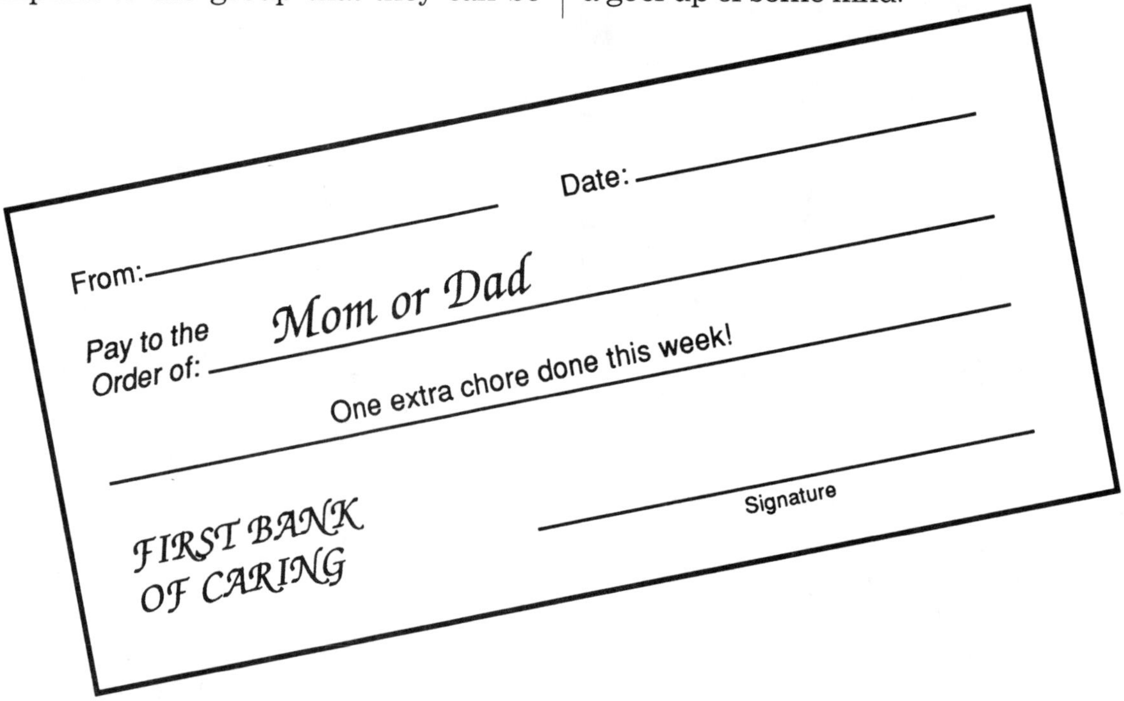

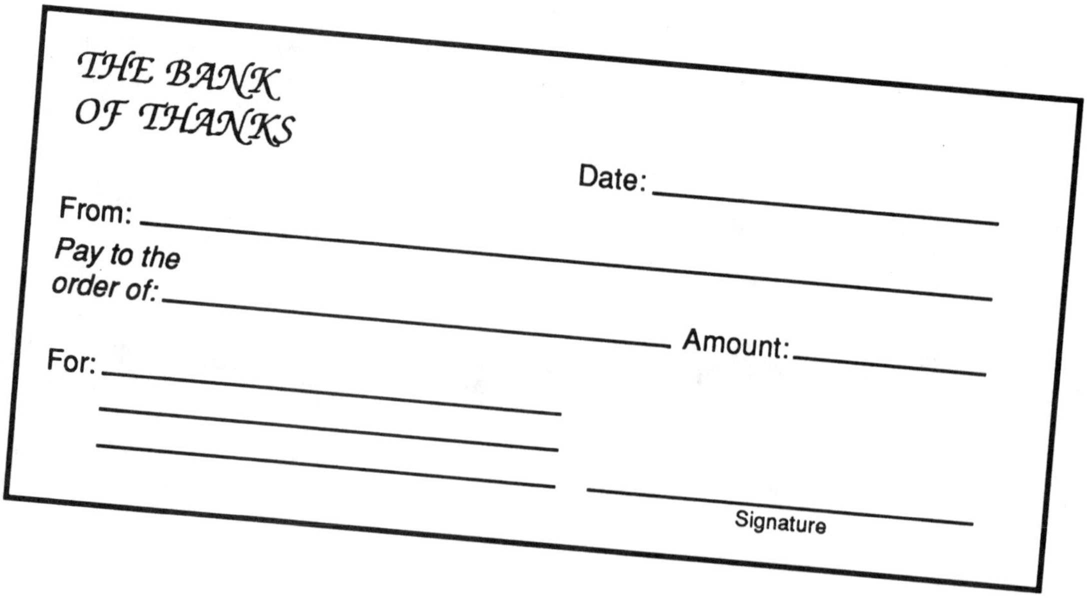

Date: _____

From: _____

Pay to the
Order of: *Mom or Dad*

One extra chore done this week!

FIRST BANK
OF CARING

Signature

THE BANK
OF THANKS

Date: _____

From: _____

Pay to the
order of: _____

Amount: _____

For: _____

Signature

Party-Making Party

Try this the next time you want to have a really unique party. Have your group put on a party for those groups you want to help. You could have a party or banquet for a retirement home, for the elderly in your congregation, for an orphanage or special education group, or for underprivileged kids. Christmas, Easter, or Thanksgiving are great times of the year for these events.

Prayer Postcard

One good way to care for the children in your group is to pray for them individually. If you do this, you might want to let them know with a personal postcard similar to the one below. Each day or week, choose one child for prayer and send a special note. Here's a sample:

Dear Jason:

Hi! Hope you are having a great week in school! You know, you are special to me and our church. I don't tell you that enough, but I want you to know it. This morning I prayed for you during my prayer and Bible study time before work. I prayed that God would be especially close to you today. God truly loves you and wants only the best for you. I do too!

In Christ,

Dave

Dave

Sandwiches for the Homeless

Canned and bulk foods are appropriate for the poor who have kitchens with ranges and ovens, but street people don't have even these. Peanut butter and jelly sandwiches, on the other hand, are inexpensive, easy to prepare, universally liked, and fairly high in nutritional value. And they freeze well.

With the guidance of your community food bank, the Salvation Army, or some other similar agency, spend a day with your group in the church kitchen or at the food bank making peanut butter and jelly sandwiches for the homeless. Solicit food from bakeries and supermarkets and let your congregation give cash gifts in order to purchase what supplies are not donated. Or ask all the members of your group to bring either jars of peanut butter or jelly (depending on the first letter of their last name). Organization for a party like this is crucial. You will need plenty of parental help. Delegate workers to provide counter space and knives, or to do clean up or delivery to the food's destination. Don't forget to write thank-you notes to those who made donations. The extra work is well worth the learning experience your group can have, especially if they and their parents get to deliver the sandwiches. Photograph the experience and make a slide presentation to your congregation.

Secret Pen Pals

Take this idea to the president of your women's organization or ladies' auxiliary. They are often looking for worthwhile projects and this one is great for breaking down barriers between generations, as well as ministering through prayer and encouragement to your kids.

Provide to your women's organization a list of all the members of your youth group, complete with names, addresses, and birthdays. Have them prepare the information on slips of paper and then have a drawing for the kids' names. Have the ladies provide gifts at Christmas, on birthdays, or on any other special time to their Secret Pen Pals, without signing their names. It will add to the excitement if the women leave monthly notes in the church office or on the bulletin board or have the gifts delivered at Sunday school time.

At the end of the year, plan a banquet given by the women's organization in honor of the young people. The ladies provide tickets for themselves, their husbands (if they are married), and their Secret Pen Pals. After a fun program, the women reveal who their pen pals have been and draw new names for the next year. The young people can be encouraged to bring gifts for their Pen Pals. During the year the kids also can leave notes of appreciation or gifts and letters on the bulletin board.

Servant Search

Here's a service project that will challenge your kids to creative servanthood. Divide your large group into small groups of three to six, with at least one responsible adult in each group. Tell them they have exactly one hour in which to go out into the community and serve in some fashion. The goal is to serve as many people as possible in any way possible. Be creative: Some groups will sweep the sidewalks, others will go door-to-door asking to wash windows or pull weeds, and others may pick up trash in a local parking lot or field. No group is allowed to receive money for the services they render.

At the end of the hour, the groups return to tell about their experiences. Discuss the different experiences and talk about what it was like to "do something for nothing." Give lots of affirmation to each team. Award teams prizes for things like the most creative service, the hardest working group, the most people served, and so on.

Thanksgiving Graffiti

Have some young people hang up and then stand by a large blank sheet of paper located in a well-traveled area of your church. The pastor should announce that after the service people are invited to write, print, or draw things that represent what they are thankful for. The young people are ready with felt-tip pens, crayons, and markers for people to use. If this activity is done early in November, the resulting graffiti can be displayed in a prominent place to remind people of how much we have to be thankful for as Thanksgiving Day approaches.

Used Bible Drive

Have you ever counted the number of Bibles in your home? Many families have several that are never read. Why not try a "Used Bible Drive" and put those extra Bibles to good use? Announce to your congregation that your group will be collecting used Bibles and other Christian reading materials to send to people who have none. Then send them to The Bible League, an organization that collects used Bibles and distributes them to other countries where they can be used. For more information about the League's program, write: The Bible League, 16801 Van Dam Rd., South Holland, IL 60473; (708) 331-2094.

Vitamin Boxes

If someone in your group (or one of their friends) is confined during a long illness, have the other group members each bring inexpensive, wrapped gifts to your next meeting. Place the gifts in a large box marked "Once-a-Day Vitamins." Deliver the box to the patient with instructions to open only one gift each day. The idea is to give the invalid something to look forward to besides treatments.

Relationship Builders

These creative caring-and-sharing experiences build positive relationships among young people and between adults and young people. They are not meant to be used as meeting starters or crowd breakers, but rather as community-building experiences.

This small group experience is fun and helps kids get to know each other better. The group is divided up into discussion groups of five to seven, and then each team is given a sheet of instructions. First, they select a team leader. The basic idea is for the groups to come up with something that they *all like* or *all dislike* in a variety of categories (see list). They are encouraged to be honest, rather than just trying to "go for the points."

For each consensus reached, the group will receive a certain number of

CATEGORY	LIKE	DISLIKE
1. Food		
2. Game		
3. TV Show		
4. Gift received		
5. School subject		
6. Chore at home		
7. Movie		
8. Hobby		
9. Way to spend Saturday		
10. Sport		
11. Toy		
12. Cartoon		
13. Bible story		
14. After-school activity		

points. You could give fifty points for any answer that everyone in the group had in common, and fewer points for answers that only some of the kids agreed on. For example, if seven kids out of a group of seven had a particular "dislike" in common, then they would get seventy points. If only five out of the same group had a "like" in common, then they would get fifty points and three people out of the seven having something in common would get thirty points.

If you wish to take this activity deeper, with the help of adults in each group, ask the members to come up with as many other shared experiences as possible. They receive additional points for each one. For example:

1. Got a "B" on the last report card.

2. Went on a backpacking trip.
3. Visited a grandparent within the last month.
4. Went trick-or-treating on Halloween night.
5. Read *Swiss Family Robinson*.
6. Read the Bible yesterday.

Give the group five to fifteen minutes to try and come up with as many of these common experiences as possible. Any experience is acceptable, as long as each person in the group has shared that experience. The team leader records as many experiences as are named by the group and agreed to. At the end of the time limit, the group can total up its points.

This exercise is an excellent relationship builder and helps kids to see just how much they have in common.

Encouragement Pennies

During a long bus trip or on a retreat, you can have some fun as well as teach your group how to encourage each other and praise one another's good deeds. First, give each group member twenty pennies. Explain to them that more pennies can be earned in the following ways:

- By giving sincere and encouraging words to other people. (Flattery—that is, giving words of praise for personal gain—is not rewarded.)
- By kind or helpful actions.
- By good attitudes while working or participating. Pennies are awarded by leaders under the following conditions:
- When leaders observe kids encouraging others by their actions, words, or attitudes.

- When young people observe encouraging actions, words, or attitudes and tell a leader about it. In this case not only the encourager but perhaps even the reporter can earn a penny.

Pennies can be confiscated by leaders under the following conditions:
- When leaders observe discouraging actions, words, or attitudes (e.g., criticizing, complaining, ridiculing, showing disrespect).
- People who receive discouraging actions, words, or attitudes may request pennies from offenders provided they:
  1. Don't reciprocate with unkind actions, words, or attitudes, and
  2. Simply smile politely and hold out their hands.

Here's what students may do when they observe discouraging actions, words, or attitudes:

1. If observers tattle to a leader, the tattletales lose a penny to the leader.
2. Before reporting offenders to a leader, the observers must ask the offenders to turn themselves in to the leader or to confess the discouraging actions, words, or attitudes to them and give up a penny.
3. If the offenders refuse at the first opportunity to admit their wrongs and give up pennies or go to a leader, then the observers may report the infractions to a leader without incurring tattletale penalties.
4. If offenders admit wrongs they lose one penny; if offenders refuse to admit guilt and are consequently reported, they lose two pennies.

To remind the kids that encouragement pays, allow the ones with the most pennies at the end of the trip or retreat to keep their pennies.

Homemade Communion

Here's a meaningful way to involve your young people in communion. After a time of prayer and a few songs, move the group into the kitchen and allow them to make their own unleavened bread. Give all of the kids jobs, from measuring ingredients to taking turns rolling the dough paper thin (keep this closely supervised).

UNLEAVENED BREAD
Cream together:
　1/4 cup sugar
　3/4 cup shortening
Mix in:
　1 teaspoon salt
　1½ cups buttermilk
　1/2 teaspoon soda
Add:
　4 to 5 cups flour

Divide the dough into four balls. Roll out the dough on a floured surface until it is wafer thin. Place the dough on greased cookie sheet. Prick it to prevent shrinkage. Bake at 450 degrees until light brown, approximately fifteen to twenty minutes.

While the bread is baking, have the kids make "wine" (grape juice). Provide a large quantity of whole, seedless grapes and let the kids crush them in a bowl, using a crushing stick. This last act can symbolize the fact that because we've sinned, we have all had a part in the crucifixion of Christ. When the grapes are all crushed, pour the juice into glasses.

Now serve communion as you normally would, using these homemade elements. It will add a great deal of meaning to this church sacrament.

Jigsaw Puzzle

Take a picture of the group and have it enlarged. Cut it up into as many pieces as there are people. Send each young person a piece of the puzzle with instructions to bring it to your next meeting. The number of pieces missing will dramatize the completeness or incompleteness of the body of Christ.

One-Pot Potluck Soup-Supper

Here's an idea that's a variation of the old friendship salad. It's an interesting way to dramatize several issues—like world hunger and how our small individual efforts can make the difference when added together and, more generally, that the meaning of the body of Christ is the union of all the gifts and individual contributions of its members.

Before the meeting, have someone boil several soup bones and add salt and herbs to make a hearty broth. This can be made well in advance and frozen, but must be thawed completely and, for best results, should be boiling rapidly at the very beginning of your meeting. Have everyone bring their favorite vegetables, like carrots or celery sticks, onions, tomatoes, or some grain or legumes, like rice or noodles, beans or barley. Each of these, in whatever small quantities, are added to the broth. Make sure you add the beans and grains first, and follow them with the vegetables, or the vegetables will get too soggy. The soup should take about one or one-and-a-half hours to cook, at a good pace. While the soup is cooking, have a movie or a speaker with the focus on world hunger or use some of the attention grabbers found in this book to dramatize further the nature of the body of Christ.

After an hour or so, serve the soup and see how amazed the kids are that their tiny offerings fit together so well to make a hearty and tasty soup.

Penny for Your Thoughts

Many times it is difficult to get kids talking in a discussion. This idea may be just the inspiration your kids need to get the verbal juices going.

Ask each of the kids to bring twenty pennies and a nickel for the next discussion (topical or general sharing of ideas). The kids sit in a circle around a plastic pot made from a child's potty chair. The leader poses a question and each person in the circle tosses in a "penny for their thoughts" on the subject. If someone wants to interject a statement (more than just a sentence), it is called "putting in their two cents worth," and the person must put in two cents. If kids cannot think of anything to say when it's their turn, they may "four-feit" by putting four cents in the pot (a person can "four-feit" only once and does so by throwing in a nickel and getting back a penny.)

When the discussion is over, give the money collected to a worthy cause.

Put-Down Potty

If you're having trouble with kids who constantly put each other down during meetings and activities, try this. Get a child's potty seat and label it the "Put-Down Potty." Write out, on a number of three-by-five cards, RESURRECTION COMPLIMENTS. Place these in the "Put-Down Potty." Then, whenever members of your group, adult or young, put down other people, they must replace the KILLER PUT-DOWN with a RESURRECTION COMPLIMENT. As a reminder to do this, when kids commit a put-down infraction, they must take three-by-five cards out of the potty and give the individuals they put down a compliment. If the put-down was directed at more than one person or at the group, the RESURRECTION COMPLIMENT can be directed to a group of people or the whole group.

This approach helps to call attention to the problem without being heavy-handed. You will discover that the increased awareness will result in fewer and fewer put-downs.

Show and Tell

From time to time, plan a "Show and Tell for the Big Kids." Invite each adult worker to bring a personal object that represents something about their feelings on life. They can bring anything (trophies, books, pictures, mementos,

poems) or share exciting experiences or answered prayers. After they share what they have brought, others in the group may ask questions. When everyone has shared, the leader should ask: (1) What new things did you learn about the people who took part in "Show and Tell?" (2) What did you all learn or relearn about yourselves?

Study Bubble

Here's something different to try with your group. Simply find two large sheets of plastic, tape them together, add a fan (an ordinary household fan will suffice) and you have a great new discussion place. It really works well, kids like it, and you can even decorate it.

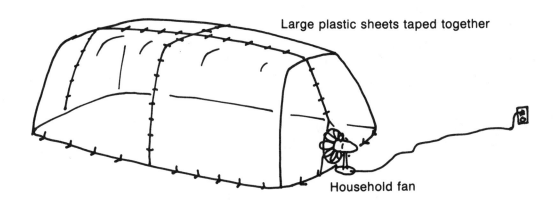

Large plastic sheets taped together

Household fan

Yarn-Sharing Experience

In order to get your kids to open up and share their inner feelings and Christian experiences, try using this technique. Assemble members in a standing circle. Take a ball of yarn (size is determined by the number of people involved) and explain to the kids that you are going to ask them to participate in a little experiment. Tell them that in a moment you are going to toss the ball of yarn (while holding onto the end so the yarn will unwind) to someone in the group. The first person to catch the ball of yarn shares one of the following (post these on the chalkboard or on newsprint where everyone can see them):
1. What God has done for them.
2. What God has done for someone they know.
3. Something they are thankful for.
4. What the group means to them.
After an individual has shared one of

the above, that person tosses the ball to someone else in the circle (while still holding onto the yarn) and the next person who catches the ball will also share one of the four things above. Keep this going until everyone in the group has had a chance to share at least once (several times is best, but this depends on the size of your group and the time you have). As the leader, you need to tell the group that you will be the first and the last person to share. That way you, and not another group member, are the person who gets picked last.

After you have made a "spider-web" pattern with the yarn and everyone has had a chance to share, stop the ball and begin to ask some questions:

1. "What is this yarn doing for us physically?" Answers will range around the idea of "holding us together." Before this you could comment that the effect of the sharing has created a beautiful web between the members of the group. You could briefly mention that for a beautiful pattern to evolve, everybody had to participate.

2. Have one or two members of the group drop hold on the yarn. Immediately the center web will become loose and the circle will widen a little. Then ask: "What happens to the group when someone drops their yarn?" (It becomes less close—looser knit—and it makes something beautiful fall apart and turn ugly.) You then could follow up with a brief talk on how the Bible teaches us to bear each other's burdens, to share our happinesses and sorrows, and to be thankful. You could really emphasize that in sharing, a beautiful network of relationships and ties is formed, just like what is physically illustrated by the yarn, but that it takes everyone to hold it together.

Group Promoters

Here you will find some creative publicity and promotion ideas designed to get your kids' attention and build up your adult leadership.

And Now for the Announcements

Those words put most listeners to sleep. Wake your group up and grab their attention with creative announcements like these:

- Play a tape recording of the announcement while the announcer lip syncs it. With practice, the announcer can mouth the words just out of sync enough with the recording so that it looks even more curious, like a foreign movie.
- Advertising an event? Hold a handful of balloons by their strings and, for every excuse that you imagine your kids would give for not attending the event, pop a balloon. End the announcement with, "If you don't come, you'll burst my bubble."
- Tape candy to fliers, then throw them out to the kids.
- Play Guy Smiley, the "Sesame Street" game-show host, and say, "Next week's event is full of surprises. Tell them what to expect, Bob." Then over the PA system, an off-camera voice—like the ones on a game show that describe the prizes—announces the event.
- Divide your group into teams. Have

them play charades with each of the announcements.

- Deliver your announcement in rap.
- During busy seasons, when you have several events to promote (summers, Decembers) over several weeks, bring a bag full of items that will visually remind your group of the event: a sleeping bag (sleep over), ski goggles (snow trip), Christmas ornament (Christmas party), hammer (service project). The second week you announce these events, all you'll have to do is pull the objects from the bag and the kids will shout the event back to you.

Announcement Treasure Hunt

If your announcements are sometimes forgotten or ignored, try an announcement treasure hunt. Divide the group into small hunting teams, and give each team a three-by-five card with one or more facts about the upcoming event on it as well as a clue that reveals where they'll find the next card.

Each group gets different cards, each with a different announcement on them. When each group has all its cards, the kids can then get the facts arranged in proper order and make the announcement to the rest of the group. This game can also be done as a relay, with one person per group chasing down each new card and returning to the group. It adds a lot of fun and excitement to announcements and helps fight those age-old excuses: "I forgot," and, "I didn't know about that."

File Cards

Most children's groups get new adult workers nearly every year. As a result, the workers rarely have time to get to know all of the kids in their group before they have to leave for some reason or another. It has been found to be extremely beneficial for the responsible children's worker to keep an up-to-date file on every regular member of the group. This file is then given to the new workers, making their job much easier. A good file is not only a bridge between workers, but it's also helpful to workers who are really interested in being aware of their group's needs—and problems. Such a file can and should be the "right arm" of an effective children's worker.

It is suggested that your file be compact, yet comprehensive. A five-by-seven file is usually sufficient, with each kid listed on a card that contains all of the following information.

1. Name, address, phone number, age, school, grade and other such facts.
2. Family information: parent's names, names of brothers and sisters, whether they are church members, and so on.
3. A picture should be included, if at all possible. One way to get a picture is just to have a "picture day" and take a photo of every kid in the group. Any picture will do, however.
4. Special information such as friends,

favorite subjects in school, special interests, and so forth.

5. On the back, an up-to-date progress report should be kept. Whenever the kid says anything significant, makes a public decision, has a counseling session, or participates in a special way,

it should be included in the file.

It's important that this file be kept as current as possible. It will enable you to be more effective in dealing with your kids on a personal, thoughtful, and responsible level.

Name

Address ___ State ___ Zip

City ___ Grade

Phone

School

Age

Parents' names

Brothers and sisters

Favorite subjects in school

Friends

Sports

Special Interests

Other Information

Place

photo

here

The Golden Apple Award

Proverbs 25:11 says, "A word aptly spoken is like apples of gold in settings of silver." So why not recognize your youth workers periodically with "The Golden Apple Award"? As the youth pastor, from time to time present a real golden apple (you can usually find them in gift shops) to one of your workers for faithful service in ministry. Let the young people themselves make the presentation during a Sunday-morning worship service, then follow up with an announcement and congratulations in the church newsletter or bulletin. Such recognitions not only honor your staff members; it also encourages them to continue and increases your ministry's visibility.

Graffiti Rules!

If you have a meeting room that is used exclusively by your group, give the kids one or two walls to graffiti with anything they want. Provide paint, spray paint, and brushes, and let the kids be creative. You might want to make a rule about public decency, but otherwise let them say what they want. You can always paint over it later and do it again.

Kid of the Week

Here is a special way to make your kids feel important and also help kids get to know each other better. Each week choose a "Kid of the Week" to be the honored guest at that week's meeting.

Here is what is involved: Contact the chosen young person's parents secretly and have them provide you with family photos, baby pictures, awards, report cards, toys, articles of clothing, or anything that would be of interest to the group. One bulletin board in the church can be set aside for the "Kid of the Week," and all those items can be hung up on the board. When the young people arrive for the meeting, they will all head straight for the "Kid of the Week" board to find out who that person is for the week. In addition, the chosen young person can be honored in some special way during the meeting. It is a good way to have fun and to let kids know that they are special.

Looking Up

If you have a difficult time getting your group to listen to announcements, here is a way to get their attention. Thumb tack or tape your announcements or posters to the ceiling. You can put them anywhere—in the hallways, youth room, or wherever kids congregate. Once someone starts looking up, pretty soon the whole group will.

Mailboxes

Give everyone in your youth group slots for their own mailbox at church. This is a convenient way to drop off flyers to your regular kids as well as a nice way for them to communicate with each other if they have special notes to give to someone. Everyone feels "important" because they have their own little niches. As you get more kids, add more mailboxes and make sure new kids are given niches as soon as possible so they get that feeling of belonging. Involve the kids in the construction and the "personalizing" of the mailboxes so they can use their creative imaginations.

Parent Questionnaire

At your next parents' meeting, have those who come fill out the questionnaire on the next page. It will help you recruit volunteer help and give you some insight into parents' perspectives on your program. Be sure to add, at the bottom, your name, address, phone number, and typical weekly schedule.

Sack Mail

You can send small, flat paper bags in the mail. Staple the open end shut and address it on one side and print your message on the other side—or enclose it in the bag. Message ideas: "Get out of the sack next Sunday morning" or "Blow this bag up and pop it . . . you'll get a bang out of our next event."

PARENT QUESTIONNAIRE

A. Personal Information
1. Name _____
2. Phone _____
3. Children in youth program:
   Name   Age   Grade   School
   _____
   _____
   _____

B. We need your help!
1. If you could provide transportation once in a while, please check here. ☐
   How many could you transport? _____
2. If you could provide refreshments one to three times this year, please check here. ☐
3. If you would be willing to offer your home as a place to meet once or twice this year, please check here. ☐
   How many people would fit comfortably? _____
   What are some special features about your home that might be of interest in planning a meeting (e.g., swimming pool, game room, wide-screen TV): _____
4. If you would be willing to assist with one of our retreats or overnighters, please check here. ☐

C. We also want to help you! Rank the discussion topics below according to how helpful they would be to you as a parent (number one being most important, and so on).
   _____ Parent-child relationships   _____ Christian models in the home
   _____ Conflict resolution   _____ On being a parent of a pre-teen
   _____ Family devotions   _____ Resources available to parents
   _____ Pressures on kids today   _____ Building a Christian home
   _____ Christian education in the home   _____ Other _____

D. Evaluation of the Childrens' Program. Please answer honestly.
1. The one thing I like best about the program is _____ .
2. The one thing I dislike about the program is _____ .
3. How do you feel about the leaders? _____
4. What one goal do you most want to see our program accomplish?
   _____

E. Please complete the following sentences:
1. God is _____ .
2. The Bible is _____ .
3. Our family is _____ .
4. The most important thing for a family to have is _____ .

F. Are there any other comments you would like to make?
   _____
   _____

Scrambled Letter

One way to make sure your young people read every line of a handout or mailer is to create a "scrambled letter." First, type your letter and number each line. Then, retype it onto a clean sheet with all of the lines scrambled. Include these instructions at the top and send it off.

Dear _____,

Why are you getting this scrambled letter? Well, read on! Each line is numbered to show you which line to read next. Find line number one and go from there.

15 like us. Oh, and if you register early (by May 31) and attend all
2 that we do things in very unconventional ways in Middle-School Vacation
5 ended up having fun. We do our own thing in our own room—even the
13 three-dimensional photo display for your room. It is really neat and
8 play games, and eat (donuts, pizza, and other yummies). Some-
1 You see, we have chosen this unusual letter to try to convince you
10 decide what). Of course, we have lessons too. That is the real meat
16 five days of VBS, you'll be eligible to win a cassette tape player.
12 even keeps the church mice listening in. Our craft this year is a
14 you can personalize it if you want. Try us—we think that you'll
4 have attended Middle School VBS before. Some of the real grumps even
7 little kids. We even do our own music. Plus . . . we go on field trips,
3 Bible School. If you don't believe us, just ask some of the kids who
9 times we bowl, play miniature golf, or go to a state park (you can help
11 of VBS, but Phil is not your ordinary boring, preacher-type and he
6 missionary comes down to us instead of us sitting up with all the

    Come join us,
    Phil Smith
    Tom Johnson
    Dave Jones

Sponsor Search

Here is a good system for recruiting adult sponsors for your group. It counteracts the two most basic objections that adults have: feeling that they don't have anything to contribute, and not knowing what is expected of them.

First, develop a booklet or series of handouts about your group, giving an overview of the ministry and spelling out exactly and specifically what advisors do. Make it simple and attractive. Next, meet with the church staff or your board to put together a "hit list" of good prospects. Be sure to have quite a few names—more than you need so that some may gracefully decline. Contact those on the list by phone or in person, asking them to consider working with the kids in your group. Emphasize that you will not need their decisions for several weeks. During this time, ask them personally to answer questions and seek to gain an impression of their commitment to Christ and their special talents and abilities. Be sure to pray together. Finally, make the decision together about their involvement. Even if the person decides not to make a long-term commitment, there are always opportunities for them to help with special events, camp counseling, and the like. Later on, they may be able to help full time.

Sticker Postcard

Here's a quick way to create your own personalized postcards to send your group members. Go to any stationery, art, or school supply store, or a Christian bookstore, and purchase a variety of stickers with positive messages like, "Good Work!" "Terrific!" "U-R-Tops!" or "God Loves You!" They are usually available individually or in rolls or sheets. Use them to add color to ordinary, drab postcards. Then add a personal note, and you have a unique way to encourage and congratulate your kids as well as thank your adult workers.

Bible Brain Teasers

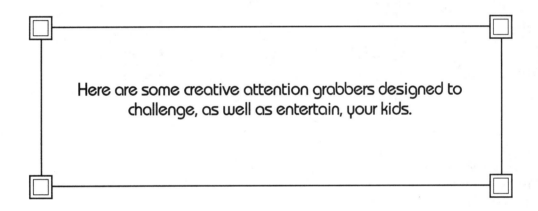

Here are some creative attention grabbers designed to challenge, as well as entertain, your kids.

This is a a word game that involves names and books of the Bible. Each kid is given the list of "clues" on page 99 and asked to write in the biblical name that fits each clue. Although it is only a game, it can help kids remember names and places in the Bible.

If your kids don't like these, have them write their own—thinking up clues can be just as much fun as solving them. Divide the kids into teams and allow each group to come up with five clues of their own. Here's how to do it: First, think of the word or name you will be using as

the answer. Second, think of what that word or name immediately brings to your mind by association, sound, or spelling. Then write a sentence that describes it and—presto!—you have a "crazy clue."

Collect the clues from all the teams. If you have time, make a master list of clues, make copies, and distribute them for everyone to solve. Otherwise, read the clues aloud, one at a time, and have each team record its answers privately. Then go through the answers together and score. Each team gets 100 points for solving a clue from any other team, and 100 points for every clue it has written that stumps the rest of the group. If the

group agrees by consensus that the unsolvable clue is misleading or poorly written, no points are awarded.

Fifteenth letter +
furniture you sleep on +
eating only selected foods

Joint of the leg +
make pants shorter
+ me + dentist
chair sound ➡

Answers:

1. Song of Solomon
2. Daniel (Dan-yell)
3. Proverbs (pro-verbs)
4. Ezra
5. Luke
6. Corinthians (core-in-the-hands)
7. Galatians (Gail-Asians)
8. Titus (tight-us)
9. Genesis (Jenny's sis)
10. Joel (Joe-will)
11. Obadiah (O-bed-diet)
12. Mark
13. Jonah
14. Timothy (timid-Thee)
15. Ruth (Babe Ruth)
16. Chronicles
17. Ezekiel (easy-kill)
18. Nahum (neigh-hum)
19. Matthew (book of New Testament)
20. Hosea (hose-ea)
21. James (Jimmy Carter)
22. Hebrews
23. Deuteronomy (due-to-Ron-and-me)
24. Lamentations (lamb-men-day-shuns)
25. Zechariah and Zephaniah (disease = "the z's")

26. Acts (ax)
27. Thessalonians (the-saloonians)
28. Kings
29. Job
30. Revelation
31. Peter (he denied Christ)
32. Exodus (exit-us)
33. Psalms (in middle of Bible)
34. Isaiah (I-say-ah)
35. Samuel (Sam-mule)
36. Micah (my-cah)
37. John (Johnny Bench)
38. Malachi (mail-a-chi)
39. Romans (Rome-ants)
40. Philemon (file-lemon)
41. Joshua (walls of Jericho)
42. Ecclesiastes (ekkly's siestas)
43. Habakkuk (a-bad-cook)
44. Amos (a-miss)
45. Numbers
46. Judges (give jail sentences)
47. Ephesians (a-fee-shuns)
48. Nehemiah (knee-hem-I-ah)
49. Philippians (Flippians)
50. Haggai (Hey guy!)

BOOKS OF THE BIBLE "CRAZY CLUES"

1. A wise king's tune. _____
2. If little Danny lets out a scream, it is a . . . _____
3. If you are not opposed to words denoting action, you are . . . _____
4. A "captive speaker" for the Jews. _____
5. Not actually hot, just _____ warm.
6. If you are holding the middle of an apple in your palms. _____
7. Two Asian women named Gail. _____
8. Ballerinas wear these on their "leg-us." _____
9. Sister to Jennifer. _____
10. Joseph agrees to do something. You could say that . . . _____
11. 15th letter + furniture you sleep on + eating only selected foods. _____
12. Right on! You really hit the . . . _____
13. A "whale" of a good book. _____
14. If a man named "Thee" was shy, he would be a . . . _____
15. Famous baseball player's last name given to him when he was just a babe. _____
16. Newspapers. _____
17. A murder that is not difficult. _____
18. The sound of a horse that forgot the words to a song. _____
19. The first of the Bible's new writers. _____
20. You water your grass-ea with a . . . _____
21. Formal first name of the U.S. president in 1978. _____
22. The Jews, the Israelites, the . . . _____
23. Ronny and I are collecting an inheritance. _____
24. A young sheep + males + not night + avoid. _____
25. Two answers: Disease of the Old Testament. _____ _____
26. You get this when you're fired. _____
27. The persons born in the old western saloons. _____
28. Higher than Queens. _____
29. An employment. _____
30. A confusing look at what lies ahead. _____
31. You can't deny this Bible writer. _____
32. When we leave. _____
33. The "central" book of the Bible. _____
34. The way a shy person might greet a stranger. _____
35. A donkey named Sammy. _____
36. How a person from Brooklyn would introduce his auto. "This is . . . " _____
37. Formal first name of a Cincinnati Red who rarely sat on the bench. _____
38. If you wanted to ship a Greek letter to someone you might . . . _____
39. What insects at picnics are called in Italy's chief city. _____
40. What file would you classify a sour yellow fruit in? _____
41. A successful demolition man. _____
42. When George Ekkly takes naps in Spain. _____
43. Not a good chef. _____
44. Not a hit. _____
45. 6 12 18 43 55 76. _____
46. People who must pronounce their sentences well. _____
47. Refusing to pay a doctor's bill. _____
48. Joint of the leg + make pants shorter + me + dentist-chair sound. _____
49. Two people born in Flippy, Montana. _____
50. If you're yelling at a strange man from across the room, you might shout . . . _____

Bible Scavenger Hunt

With the help of their Bibles, players must decode the numbers to determine what it is they have to find. Here is the decoder.

For example, 1 - 1 - 37 - 3 - 29 means Old Testament, Genesis (the first book), chapter 37, verse 3, and the 29th word in the verse—that is, a robe. This example

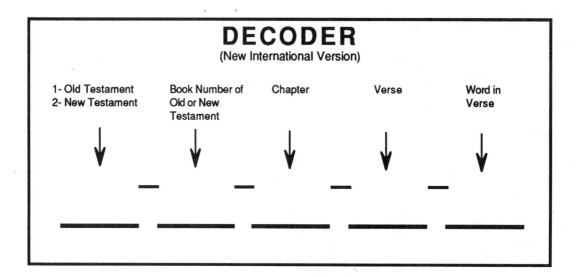

was taken from *The New International Version.* Be sure your kids use only the version that you design the code around. For starters (in *The New International Version)* you can send your kids after salt (1 -1-19 - 26 - 12), bush (1 - 2 - 3 - 2 - 17), leprosy (2 - 3 - 5 - 12 - 17), and scrolls (2 - 16 - 4 - 13 - 16).

Bible "What's the Meaning?" Riddle

On the following page is a Bible brain teaser that is fun but challenging for kids to try and figure out. After doing this one your group may want to write their own. The object, of course, is to look at the arrangements of letters, numbers, or objects and guess the words or phrases that interpret each one.

(Answers: 1. Rejoice in the Lord. 2. He spoke to them in parables. 3. Go down Moses. 4. Whosoever believes in me. 5. Believe on the Lord Jesus Christ. 6. Victory over sin and death. 7. Justification by faith. 8. Narrow way. 9. Spreading the gospel. 10. Rightly dividing the word of truth. 11. Paradise. 12. No room in the inn.)

Bible Brain Teasers

1. LO ᴿᴱᴶᴼᴵᶜᴱ RD

2.   BULL
HE SPOKE TO THEM
      BULL

3. M
   O
     S
       E
         S

4. M ᵂᴴᴼˢᴼᴱⱽᴱᴿ ᴮᴱᴸᴵᴱⱽᴱˢ E

5.   BELIEVE
LORD JESUS CHRIST

6.   VICTORY
SIN DEATH

7. JUSTIFICATION/FAITH

8.

9. g o s p e l

10. WO RD
   O F
TR UTH

11. DICE
DICE

12. HOROOMTEL
MOROOMTEL
INN

Mindbenders

Mental games are wonderful fun even if your kids can't always figure them out—adults can't either! Introduce one now and then to challenge your group's thinking skills. Pace yourself with Mindbenders, as they tend to take a little longer than other types of attention grabbers.

Abdul the Magnificent

This is a mind-reading stunt that, when done correctly, is downright spooky. Give everyone slips of paper and ask them to write short sentences on them. The slips are then folded, collected, and "Abdul" (who can be dressed appropriately) proceeds to perform the task of reading the sentences to the group without opening the papers.

How is it done? Abdul also puts one slip of paper in the box along with the others, only he puts some kind of identifying mark on his. When the reading starts, he picks one of the slips from the box, rubs it on his forehead without opening it, and offers any sentence as a guess as to what is on the paper. He then looks at the paper and, to his dismay he is wrong, but that will soon be forgotten. He can blame it on the fact that he was not concentrating well enough yet, but would do better on the next one. It's important not to dwell long on this mistake. Just move on to the next one. It also is important not to reveal what was actually on the paper that was guessed incorrectly. Another slip of paper is held to the forehead, and Abdul then repeats

the sentence that was actually on the previous slip of paper. After rubbing his forehead, he opens this second slip of paper, confirms that he is correct, and asks the person who wrote that sentence to identify it. Everyone is impressed. Another paper is drawn and again, Abdul repeats the sentence that was on the previously opened slip. Each time he opens up a slip of paper to see if he is "correct," he is actually learning the next sentence. The important thing is to stay one slip ahead. When he comes to his own slip, which has been held until last, he repeats the sentence on the previous slip, and that takes care of all of them. If this is done smoothly, it will really baffle the group.

Bang, You're Dead

This is a game in which the leader knows the "secret" and the rest of the group tries to guess how it's done. Everyone should be seated around the room in a casual manner, with the leader at the front. After everyone is quiet, the leader raises one hand, points it like a gun, and says "Bang, you're dead." The leader then asks the group to guess who was shot. It's hardly ever the person who was being pointed at. Several people will guess, and they will most likely be wrong. Then you announce who it was that you actually shot. You do it several times, changing what you do each time to throw people off, but each time pointing a finger at someone and saying, "Bang, you're dead." People try to guess, and then you announce who it really was. Make sure that they understand that it is possible to know right away who it is that has been shot, but they have to figure out what the "secret" or "clue" is.

And just what is the secret? The person who actually was shot is the first person to speak after you say "Bang, you're dead." Sooner or later, someone will catch on as you perhaps make it a little more obvious. It's fun as well as frustrating.

Baseball Baffler

Here is a fun quiz that might be useful during baseball season or whenever you choose. The object is to identify the twenty-six major league baseball teams by the clues given on the next page.

BASEBALL BAFFLER

1. Civil War faction _____
2. "Father's" team _____
3. Jack's beanstalk adversary _____
4. Catholic officials _____
5. Tea makers _____
6. Indian warriors _____
7. Big cats _____
8. All "stars" _____
9. Bright stockings _____
10. Communists _____
11. Apaches, Comanches, Navajos _____
12. Army-draft avoiders _____
13. Colored letters _____
14. Boy Scout group _____
15. Ornithologist's favorite _____
16. Alphabet beginners _____
17. "Encountered" group _____
18. Park keepers _____
19. Blackbeard's crew _____
20. Clean hosiery _____
21. Exhibitions or displays _____
22. Heavenly team _____
23. "Kings" of the game _____
24. Young mares _____
25. Seafaring men _____
26. Double trouble _____

Answers:

1. New York Yankees
2. San Diego Padres
3. San Francisco Giants
4. St. Louis Cardinals
5. Milwaukee Brewers
6. Atlanta Braves
7. Detroit Tigers
8. Houston Astros
9. Boston Red Sox
10. Cincinnati Reds
11. Cleveland Indians
12. Los Angeles Dodgers
13. Toronto Blue Jays
14. Chicago Cubs
15. Baltimore Orioles
16. Oakland A's
17. New York Mets
18. Texas Rangers
19. Pittsburgh Pirates
20. Chicago White Sox
21. Montreal Expos
22. California Angels
23. Kansas City Royals
24. Philadelphia Phillies
25. Seattle Mariners
26. Minnesota Twins

Color Crazy

Have several colored areas (red, blue, green) on a poster board. On each colored area, write the name of a color, but not the actual color of that area of the poster. Then, for a gag, have the kids try to name the colors on the poster as you point to them—not the words written, but the actual colors. It's not easy.

Crazy Grams

Break your young people into groups of three. Each team needs to be given a sheet of paper and a pencil. Randomly call out four to fifteen letters of the alphabet (the more letters, the more difficult the task). One of the team members will need to be appointed team recorder to write the called-out letters across the piece of paper given them. Each team now tries to create a message out of the letters that were called out. For example, suppose you called out the letters H, M, F, F, D, a team's crazy gram could read:

"Help My Feet Feel Dizzy!"

or

"Having More Fun Feeding Donkeys!"

Let the groups read their crazy grams out loud after each round. Award every group a winner with categories like the funniest, the most creative, the silliest, or the weirdest.

Crossword People

Divide the group into teams of equal size with twelve to twenty-four kids on each team. Have each team select a captain who will keep order and direct the team. Prepare ahead of time sets of alphabet letters on twelve-inch-square cards that team members hang around their necks. Each team should have identical sets of letters, consisting of frequently used vowels and consonants, plus two or three rarely used letters such as Q, X, or Z. At a signal, each team tries to form a "crossword" puzzle, using as many members of the team as possible, within a given time limit. For example: Using the letters PGNOOFYECA JAXTIIUM, a team could line up this way:

Award points to the team that uses the

most members, makes the longest word, the most words, and so forth. Another idea would be to assign point value to each letter and add points up as if you were playing a game of "Scrabble."

"Is It This?"

This game is a simple and fun mind-bender. Clue one of your group members in before you begin: tell that person the key word is *that* and explain the game. Ask the clued-in volunteer to leave the room. The group then chooses an object. Ask the volunteer to return to the room. Instruct the volunteer to guess what object the group has selected. Do this by pointing to various objects and asking, "Is it this ____?" When you point to an object and say, "Is it that ____?" your clued-in volunteer will know you have pointed to the selected object and can answer correctly.

For example, if your group selected the piano, your directions to the clued-in person could go something like this:

Leader: "Is it this eraser?"
Volunteer: "No."
Leader: "Is it this chair?"
Volunteer: "No."
Leader: "Is it this song book?"
Volunteer: "No."
Leader: "Is it that piano?"
Volunteer: "Yes!"

Knife, Fork, and Spoon Game

This is a simple "mind reading" game and yet one that can take up a good deal of time, depending upon the alertness of the participants. To play, you will need a knife, a fork, and a spoon. Have the kids sit in a circle on the floor. Explain the game (secretly) to another person and begin.

Send your partner out of the room and tell the kids that they should pick someone sitting in the circle. Then tell them that you will communicate with your partner by what you do who was chosen to be "It." Place the knife, fork, and spoon in any arrangement you choose on the floor in the middle of the circle, and then pick a place in the circle to sit. The key to communicating who is "It" to your partner has nothing to do with the knife, fork, and spoon, but the fact that you assume a sitting position exactly like that of "It." If "It" moves to a different position to be more comfortable, so do you. Your partner makes a big deal about the knife, fork, and spoon, but picks up the clues from what you do, which is what you told the kids in your initial instruction. The knife, fork, and spoon are merely diversionary because the kids assume what you do is limited to the knife, fork, and spoon. After your partner picks "It"—to the total amazement of the group—the process is repeated until someone catches on. If someone feels they know the answer, they then go out of the room and become your partner. Depending upon the alertness of the group, this can continue until everyone has had a chance to figure out the key to the game.

Name Train

This is a great memory mindbender. Ask your kids to sit in a circle. One person starts by giving his name. Moving clockwise the person to the left then introduces herself to the group as well as the first person. Continuing clockwise, the next person introduces himself to the group as well as the second and first persons. As you can see, the farther around the circle you move, the greater the memory test. If you have a large group, you may want to break into teams of ten or so to make it a little easier.

Number Nonsense

Here are several tricks that are easy to do, will seem baffling to the kids in your group, and make you appear to be a genius. Try them sometime just for fun. It's best to memorize each procedure so it looks like you do it all the time.

Choose a Number:
Suggest that someone in your group (or the entire group) secretly choose a number between ten and 100. This number is not to be told to the leader. The leader proceeds to find out what the number is. Let's say that the number is 44.

Number selected	44
Double it	88
Add 1	89
Multiply by 5	445
Add 5	450
Multiply by 10	4,500

The leader now subtracts 100 from the result without saying anything. Thus 100 from 4,500 is 4,400. Strike off the last two digits and announce the number is 44.

The Age of the Change in Your Pocket:
Have someone in your group think of their age (without telling anyone). Have them double it, and then add five, and then multiply by fifty. Now add to that number the amount of pocket change in someone else's pocket. Now have them subtract the number of days in a year from that number. At this point the number can be disclosed to the entire group. To this number, the leader secretly adds 115. The age of the person will be the first two digits. The amount of change will be indicated by the last two digits.

The person's age	15
Double the person's age	30
Add 5	35
Multiply by 50	1,750
Add pocket change (37 cents)	1,787
Subtract 365 days in the year	1,422
(This number is given to the group)	
Secretly add 115	1,537

The leader announces that the age is 15 and the amount of change in the pocket is 37 cents.

When Was I Born?:
Announce that you can guess the age and the month of birth of anybody in the group and give the volunteer the following instructions:

Write down the number of the month you were born

August	8
Double it	16
Add 5	21
Multiply by 50	1,050
Add your age (16)	1,066

Subtract the number of days in
a year (365)   701

Call for the result; secretly add 115, which makes the total 816. Immediately announce August as the month of birth and 16 as the age. The first one or two digits indicate the month and the last two indicate the age.

Secret Number:
This simple trick is fun as the kids try to figure it out. Ask someone to select a number, keeping it a secret. Now ask that person to double it, then to multiply by five, and then to tell you the total. Immediately you are able to tell that individual the secret number. All you have to do is to knock off the final digit, for what you have really done is to get the number multiplied by ten. Example: The number selected is 13. Multiplied by 2 it is 26. Multiplied by 5 it is 130. Knock off the last digit and it is 13, the secret number. This may be worked on a crowd with the teller staying outside the room while the group decides on the secret number.

Picture Search

Borrow a 35mm camera (or a photographer with a 35mm camera) and stroll around inside your church building, photographing both familiar and not-so-familiar objects from unusual angles. Close-up and wide-angle lenses are helpful. How many people know what the back of the pulpit looks like? How about the inside of the janitor's closet?

When the photos are printed, post them on a bulletin board with identifying numbers. Then give each of the kids a simplified copy of the floor plans of the church building. Instruct them to figure out where in the church each photo was taken, then to write the photo's number in the corresponding area of the floor plans. The student with the most correct locations wins. Common objects can be the most difficult to identify. You can make the game more challenging by using black-and-white film instead of color.

Smell the Broom

Two people need to know in advance how this game works, you and a volunteer. Brag to the audience about your keen sense of smell. To prove it, have a broom brought in and have it given to the other person to hold parallel to the floor in both hands. Leave the room while the broom holder asks someone from the audience to touch the broom handle anyplace he or she chooses. When this is done, come in to sniff back and forth across the broom handle to "smell out" the spot where the person touched it. Move your nose across the handle while looking at the holder's feet. The holder should have shoes on. When your nose crosses the spot where the broom was touched, the holder moves his toes on one foot up and down very slightly to indicate to you that your nose just crossed the spot that was touched. The smeller now knows where the spot is and can point to it and ask if the audience wants to try again. A lot of fun can be had with this game since the movement of the shoe is so slight that the audience cannot detect it.

Sum Fun

Divide the group into teams and give each person a copy of the list below. Each phrase has a corresponding number that should be written in the space provided. then, the numbers should be added up to get a "total." The team that is first to get the correct total is the winner. Teams can trade information if they want. Pocket calculators can be provided to make the addition a little easier, or they can be outlawed to make it a little tougher.

```
                        SUM FUN
  1. Letters in the alphabet.                    _____
  2. Wonders of the ancient world.               _____
  3. Signs of the Zodiac.                        _____
  4. Cards in a deck (with jokers).              _____
  5. Planets in the solar system.               _____
  6. Piano keys.                                 _____
  7. Baker's dozen.                              _____
  8. Holes on a golf course.                     _____
  9. Degrees in a right angle.                   _____
 10. Sides on a stop sign.                       _____
 11. Quarts in a gallon.                         _____
 12. Hours in a day.                             _____
 13. Wheels on a unicycle.                       _____
 14. Digits in a zip code.                       _____
 15. Varieties in Heinz.                         _____
 16. Players on a football team.                 _____
 17. Words that a picture is worth.              _____
 18. Days in February in a Leap Year.            _____
 19. Squares on a checkerboard.                  _____
 20. Days and nights of the great flood.         _____
 21. Leagues under the Sea.                      _____
 22. Days in a work week.                        _____
 23. Digits in a social security number.         _____
         Total:                                  _____
```

Answers to Sum Fun:

1. 26	7. 13	13. 1	19. 64
2. 7	8. 18	14. 5	20. 40
3. 12	9. 90	15. 57	21. 20,000
4. 54	10. 8	16. 11	22. 5
5. 9	11. 4	17. 1,000	23. 9
6. 88	12. 24	18. 29	

Total: 21,574

That's the Fact, Jack

Give your group a copy of the following story. Have them read it within a two-minute time limit. When time is up, have them turn the page over and answer the questions that follow. Give a prize to the person who gets the most questions right.

THAT'S THE FACT, JACK

The Story:

An elderly woman with young blue eyes saw an old man who was blue sitting on a light brown bench. His name was Black and he was green with illness. As the woman, who looked very young to Black, approached, he rose to his feet and asked her a question.

"I ate a sandwich that made me ill. Can you help me find a doctor . . . ?"

"Why do you need a doctor? You don't look sick to me!"

"But I am sick. I'm green. I can't even make it across the street."

"There's no street here. Only this long road and very short pathway."

"Just get out of my way, so I can make a long path to the shortest road into town."

He rose, walked to the road, and was hit by a grey truck moving at 84,263 miles per hour. Now he really was sick!

The Questions:
1. Was the woman young or old?
2. Did the man have blue eyes?
3. Where was the man sitting?
4. What color was the thing he sat on?
5. What was the man's name?
6. What did the man ask the woman to help him find?
7. Besides being sick, what physical problem did the man have?
8. Was the road they were on long or short?
9. Was the pathway they were on long or short?
10. How did the man die?
11. What color was the truck?

Writing in the Sand

Here is a "mind reading" game in which the leader and a partner try to baffle the rest of the group. The group selects a secret word and the partner comes in and is able to guess the word correctly following a short series of clues from the leader, which the group tries to figure out.

The leader holds a stick in her hand, and appears to "write in the sand" some clues. The writing does not appear to make sense, however, and bears no obvious relationship to the secret word being guessed. But the partner is still able to guess the word on the first try.

Here is how it's done: The consonants in the word (say the secret word is light) are L, G, H, and T. These are given to the

---

partner through a series of verbal clues after entering the room. The leader might first say, "Let's see if you can get this one." The first letter of that sentence is "L." That would clue the partner that the word starts with an "L." Then, the leader draws on the floor with the stick, and at some point taps out either one, two, three, four, or five taps. These are the vowels. "A" is one tap, "U" is five taps.

So, in this case, the leader would tap the stick three times for "I." Now the partner has two letters. The "G" is given next with a verbal clue, like "Got it yet?"

As soon as the partner has enough letters to guess the word, she does and amazes the group. Then kids who think they know how it is done may try their skill as the partner.

Yarn Guess

This is one of those things you do just for fun. On one side of the room put some numbers on the wall (on cards or just write on the wall). Attach to each number the end of a long piece of yarn. Then hang the yarn up the wall, across the ceiling, and down the opposite wall to a letter on the wall. Let the yarn make a few turns, go through things, and so on, to make it interesting. With about twenty-five different lengths of yarn going across the room connecting numbers and letters, it really looks wild. The object is to have the kids try to figure out which number connects up with which letter. Whoever guesses the most wins a prize.